THE ACADEMIC STUDY OF JUDAISM

Essays and Reflections

THE ACADEMIC STUDY OF JUDAISM

Essays and Reflections

JACOB NEUSNER

Professor of Religious Studies
Brown University

KTAV PUBLISHING HOUSE, INC.
1975

Library of Congress Cataloging in Publication Data

Neusner, Jacob, 1932-
  The academic study of Judaism.

  Includes bibliographical references.
  1. Jewish learning and scholarship—United States—
Addresses, essays, lectures. 2. Jewish studies—United
States—Addresses, essays, lectures. I. Title.
DS113.N37   296'.07   75-5782
ISBN 0-87068-281-4

MANUFACTURED IN UNITED STATES OF AMERICA

TABLE OF CONTENTS

For

Arnold J. Band

PREFACE

For the past fifteen years I have participated in the discussion of issues and problems of the academic study of Judaism, particularly in Departments of Religious Studies, as part of the much wider discussion of "Jewish studies," in their many forms, in universities. Many of these discussions took the form of lectures at academic meetings and elsewhere; some of them appeared in various magazines, newspapers, books, and scholarly journals. Among these printed papers are a few which I hope may be of interest beyond the occasion for which they were originally prepared. It is these few papers which I have selected for the present volume, the first eight. The last two are public addresses; in introducing them, I explain why, despite their pertinence only briefly and at one specific occasion, I have included them.

While I have made minor corrections in the papers, I have not revised them. Rather, I have added to each a critique, meant to discuss the issue of the foregoing paper from a different angle, to criticize the theses advanced in the paper, and otherwise to make possible a broad-gauged discussion. Preparing these critiques was the source of much pleasure to me, not to mention a measure of merriment. I have no need to argue that I in particular was right in particular about some particular issue. It is far more interesting to me to re-open issues and advance inquiries begun a while ago, to test propositions against new experience, to reshape theses in response to the arguments of other reasonable people. In addition to the appended comments, set in italics to distinguish them from the original paper, I also explain, in the introductions to each section, the purposes and settings pertinent to the writing of the several essays therein contained.

Accordingly, I offer these essays in company with reflections about, and searching criticisms of them. In this way I hope to advance discussion of the issues and problems, the propositions and theses, offered here, always trying to show several sides of a given problem, to allow the issues, not the specific proposals of a given paper, to come to the fore. Perhaps this novel mode of presenting ideas for discussion will prove fruitful. Experience in the very new setting for the very old tradition of Jewish learning accumulates, and we recognize more clearly than before the intellectual and scholarly requirements of this new circumstance.

Throughout these essays I find myself arguing for something, against something. There is a pugnacious and polemical spirit in them. At some points I mean to apologize for the need for polemic. But it is not the personality of this writer that generates that necessity. It is, rather, the curious concatenation of three facts: the novelty of the setting; the deep resentments expressed by Jewish scholars of Judaism in Jewish seminaries and other schools of higher learning toward the university professors of "Jewish studies" in their several forms; and the tendency, on the part of the greater number of Jewish scholars of Jewish studies, wherever they are located, to analyze issues—when they do at all—in private and in terms of personalities. The pettiness and small-minded discourse which pass for criticism extend even to common problems, shared by all, and failings characteristic of all. In presenting these essays to colleagues for their criticism, I offer for discussion sharply defined viewpoints on these common issues and problems. Perhaps we may thereby transform griping, backbiting, and sniping into constructive criticism, joined to significant, concrete achievement in education and scholarship. For the most effective criticism is superior accomplishment, which should (but does not) silence backbiting and vilification, not to mention polemic.

These papers originated as follows:

University Studies in Minority Cultures, *The Journal of Higher Education,* Vol. XXXV, No. 4, April, 1964, pp. 202-206.

Jewish Studies in the American University, *The Journal of General Education,* Vol. XIII, No. 3, October, 1961, pp. 160-166.

Classical Judaism and the Intellect, The Edgar J. Goodspeed Lecture, Denison University, Granville, Ohio, November 4, 1974.

Two Settings for Jewish Studies, *YIVO Annual of Jewish Social Science,* Vol. XV (N.Y., 1974), pp. 204-224.

The Study of Religion as the Study of Tradition in Judaism, *History of Religions,* February, 1975. First presented as a lecture at the Symposium on Methodology and World Religions, School of Religion, University of Iowa, April 16, 1974.

Modes of Jewish Studies in the University, *The Study of Religion in Colleges and Universities,* ed. Paul Ramsey and John F. Wilson (Princeton, 1970: Princeton University Press), pp. 159-189.

Graduate Education in Judaica: Problems and Prospects, *Journal of the American Academy of Religion,* Vol. XXXVII, No. 4, December, 1969, pp. 321-330. First presented as the Presidential Address at the annual meeting of the American Academy of Religion, Boston, Massachusetts, on October 24, 1969.

Autodidacts in Graduate School, *Association for Jewish Studies Newsletter,* No. 8, February, 1973, pp. 4, 6. First presented in a panel discussion, The Nature and Structure of Judaic Studies in the Graduate School, Association for Jewish Studies meeting, University of Maryland, November 13, 1972.

Creativity in the Context of Judaism. Address to Anshe Emet Synagogue, Chicago, Illinois, on the occasion of receiving the Solomon Goldman Award for Jewish Creativity, October 27, 1974.

To the Class of 1976. Address to Brown University Class of 1976, September, 1972.

Copyrights are held as follows:

University Studies in Minority Cultures. © 1964 by the Ohio State University Press, Columbus, Ohio. Reprinted by permission.

Jewish Studies in the American University. © 1961 by the Pennsylvania State University. Reprinted by permission.

The Study of Religion as the Study of Tradition in Judaism. © 1975 by the University of Chicago Press. Reprinted by permission.

Modes of Jewish Studies in the University. © 1970 by Princeton University Press. Reprinted by permission.

Graduate Education in Judaica: Problems and Prospects. © 1969 by the American Academy of Religion. Reprinted by permission.

I thank the several copyright-holders for permission to reprint my papers in this volume.

This book is dedicated to one of those academic scholars in the field of Jewish studies who has shaped the thinking of all of us, who has given me, at crucial times, important and critical counsel, and who in addition is a major scholar. But the dedication is primarily a gesture of friendship and affection, not only admiration.

J.N.

PRELIMINARY OBSERVATIONS

Introduction

The first two papers present a case for the inclusion of "Jewish studies" in the university curriculum. The most general comes first: the curriculum is inappropriately limited to a narrow range of cultures, histories, and literatures, and ignores the interests of students⁄ who derive from other than Northwestern Europe. The second, on "Jewish studies," argues that such studies contain worthwhile information and insight. Obviously, after fifteen years, one must define issues for discussion in a quite different way. Since "Jewish studies" and the study of a wide range of human experience now find a natural place within the curriculum of the better universities, we no longer need to argue that they should be accepted. The outsider, looking in, has to make a case for admission, appealing to the noblest and most rational traits of the very people who have kept him out. That, in essence, is the spirit of these early papers.

Was it appropriate to the time, and is it appropriate today? The answer to the second question is surely negative. What is demanded of "Jewish studies" is to be at least as intelligent as any other field—but no more so. Each university attracts its appropriate clientele, and for each, a certain level of intellectual sophistication and scholarly attainment is to be reached, that but no higher, if also no lower. When we look back to the late 1950s and early 1960s, when only a very few positions in "Jewish studies" existed, and these at the most prestigious universities, we may conclude that it did not do much harm to advocate the inclusion of that area, but probably did not do much good either. It was not arguments such as these which led to the creation of academic positions in the wide range of Jewish learning but, I believe, three facts.

7

First, on the side of Departments of Religious Studies, many such departments by the early 1960's had reached the point at which the absence of the study of Judaism was noteworthy and regretted. Jewish students naturally expressed a certain interest in the study of Judaism, but so too did faculty, for instance, in the field of New Testament or Tanakh, and so too did students who simply wanted to study about Western religions other than Christian ones. On the side of Departments of Near Eastern Studies, positions in Hebrew, as part of the study of Semitic languages, were a natural extension of existing curricular requirements. A greater professionalism led to the preference, for instruction in Hebrew, of full-time and well-trained people, in place of local rabbis holding in-service doctorates from Jewish seminaries. Both of these developments were generated within the departments and in accord with natural growth of curricula.

A second reason for the development of new positions was simply the prosperity of the 1960's, coupled with the recognition that Jewish students formed an important part of the constituency of universities. It was both possible and judicious, therefore, to expand in this area. This development derived chiefly from administrations, so far as I can tell.

A third reason, toward the end of the 1960's, was the development of what is called "ethnic self-consciousness" and requires no comment. Each group saw others finding places for themselves in the firmament of the university curriculum and demanded the same for itself. While it has been estimated that nearly half of all positions have been financed by the organized Jewish community, it is difficult to think of more than a few significant and permanent positions founded upon such a basis. It was not parents' money but students' interest which encouraged departments and administrations to consider "Jewish studies." It also was not reasoned arguments, such as those attempted in these papers. I do not believe many of those who ultimately made the decisions to create the various positions which came into being heard arguments such as are presented here, or, if they did, cared.

I

UNIVERSITY STUDIES IN MINORITY CULTURES

Fifty years ago, most European and several Asian languages and cultures were understood by groups of Americans. Today many of these same languages and cultures have to be studied in government programs, because in the intervening time America has succeeded in blotting out the remnants of its newer-immigrant cultures. Apart from the obvious political loss, which has been recognized by the government, there is a deeper misfortune. American society would have profited from the presence in its midst of diverse and interesting ethnic groups, each preserving its own manners and customs, all providing Americans with a broad series of options in cultural and social affairs. Today, the lowest common denominator in society is usually the radically isolated individual who has few meaningful group ties and no significant inherited culture apart from the shallowest stratum of that of the common society. All too few of the older immigrant groups have succeeded in transmitting their heritage to, or beyond, the third generation. The obvious exception to this rule is in religion; yet even here, the outlines of the common American religious faiths are more clearly discerned than the distinguishing, authentic characteristics of specific, unique historical-religious cultures.

I believe this to be a self-evident loss for American civilization. Variety among men is, in my opinion, always more interesting and appealing than uniformity, just as diversity in ideas and patterns of behavior, within broad limits, is the richest source of self-questioning, growth, and change for complacent persons.

American universities have made a significant contribution to the preservation of the broad variety of social, ethical, and cultural alternatives available to modern men from distant places and every age. They have done so because that is their task in liberal education. The consequence is that at least some cultures are taught thoroughly and well. They include those of Britain, France, Germany, Spain, Latin America and, most recently, Russia. The reasons that these countries are studied in preference to other equally interesting ones are obvious: Except in the case of France and Russia, large numbers of Americans have in recent times visited them, or, as in the case of German, need a given language in research. The traditional attractiveness of French, a language once regarded as essential for all educated men, has been reinforced in recent times by the appeal of French culture for sophisticated Americans; and even more recently, Italian has achieved some popularity for the same reason. The new emphasis on Russian studies (which will probably soon extend to Chinese studies) springs from obvious political reasons. Two other cultures, those of ancient Greece and Rome, are widely studied because of their traditional place in the inherited curriculum.

A case may be made for the proposition that one region, literature, or culture is intrinsically more interesting and important than another. Those who make it, however, are generally more familiar with the culture and literature they wish to propagate than any other. Thus the teacher of a foreign language comes quite seriously to believe, from long knowledge and deep appreciation of it, that no one who is ignorant of his special subject can regard himself as literate. Indeed, the language teacher who did not regard his subject as intrinsically interesting would not be effective. On the other hand, such a proposition might be more convincing if its proponent had some significant grounds for comparison; for, after all, he is asking assent to a comparative judgment. Normally, however, proponents of one of the accepted languages exhibit little more than shallow parochialism in their advocacy. They regard their home city—whether it be Rome or Athens or Paris—as the center of the world, and therefore of education. The obvious corollary is that Warsaw, Stockholm, Teheran, or Jerusalem is relegated to the cultural periphery, and the achievements of men in those places are regarded as somehow not interesting or significant for society as a whole. But why is Athens considered more central than Jerusalem, or Paris more central than Warsaw or Dublin? This is the question that needs to be answered if we are to ignore in the curriculum the achievements of men in Warsaw, Dublin, or Jerusalem.

One may question on two counts whether the present emphasis on the normative cultures and languages ought to bar other contemporary and ancient languages from the curriculum. First of all, to allow it to do so is to ignore the deep personal interest of numerous Americans in countries other than France, Britain, and Germany. It assumes, as have American educators for far too long, that most Americans come from northwestern European countries and share the traditions of the Anglo-Saxons. It also implies that what matters in northwestern Europe happens in Britain, France, and Germany; for Holland, Sweden, Norway, and Denmark are as little known in general history courses, and as unrepresented in language departments, as Afghanistan or Tibet. Yet Swedish-Americans, and Polish-Americans, and Italian-Americans, even to the third generation, continue to concern themselves with the countries of their forefathers. Is this a more parochial interest than that of British-Americans? Moreover, 10 percent of the American people are of African descent, and have a hunger, too long unsatisfied, to know more about African history, languages, literature, music, and art. Large numbers of Americans come from southeast European countries: Poland, Hungary, Czechoslovakia, the Balkans, and Greece. They have practically no opportunity to study these countries in most universities.

Second, the emphasis on a few countries to the exclusion of others perpetuates a cultural parochialism that is peculiarly inappropriate in the contemporary world, and results in literary and historical ignorance of vast groups of mankind that have become no less important than Western Europeans. India, China, and Japan are practically excluded from the cultural experience of students at most American colleges and universities, though this situation is gradually changing. In general, however, students interested in these countries, all of which have had long and exciting histories and have produced substantial literatures available in translation, simply must study on their own or with amateurs who lack substantial qualifications for teaching.

The emphasis in academic studies of religion is likewise extraordinarily narrow. The history of Christianity dominates the liberal-arts curriculum, even in secular institutions, by governing the selection of pre-modern subjects to be studied. Yet that history is taught mainly from the perspective of American Protestantism. Western Latin Christianity is studied up to the Reformation, Protestant Christianity after it. The Council of Trent marks the dividing line in numerous general-education courses in Western history, for example: before that time there were Christians; afterward, there were Protestants—and the Roman Catholics fade from the scene. Thus Aquinas is read, Newman is not. Moreover, orthodox Christianity and the Eastern churches are practically ignored from the beginning, even though for the first three centuries of Christian history, and long afterward, they dominated the faith. The Byzantine church is ignored, its writers unread, its rite and liturgy unexplored. Only those wholly ignorant of its treasures could advance the argument that the reason is lack of religious achievement. Another example is that of Armenian Christianity, which embodies the history of Armenia. Close to one-half million Armenians in the U.S.A. preserve their religion, rites, literature, music, and a folk-culture of extraordinary color and grace. Their history as a Middle Eastern people, like that of Poland in eastern Europe, records incredible perseverance and endurance; the Huguenots of the East, the Armenians, simply do not exist in most university curriculums.

My argument is, to repeat, that Americans who are not Western Europeans deserve a far greater opportunity to study their own ethnic and cultural origins than they receive at present in our universities; and, moreover, I maintain that providing this opportunity will significantly broaden and deepen the viewpoint of Americans engaged in the study of the humanities.

It will be contended, and I wholly agree, that the chief role of the universities is to preserve and enhance American civilization, and that civilization is recorded primarily in British, French, and German literature. No one argues that Polish should supplant French, or Armenian, German, in our universities. French and German do exert a greater influence on our minds than Polish or Armenian. It seems to me quite reasonable, however, to suggest that our universities need to broaden their cultural horizons, and that even in a small institution it should be recognized that major and minor studies can be accommodated in the same curriculum, just as specialized and general-education courses are.

How ought this to be done?

First, by broadening graduate education, it should be possible for a larger number of scholars in the humanities and social sciences to master a second subject, say history or language, in which they might be competent to teach general-education or undergraduate courses in addition to their special field. As the result, one might hope to find a man qualified to teach Byzantine and also Armenian studies; or Russian and also Polish or Czechoslovak history and literature, even in translation. Such men might aspire to no more than minimal competence in the minor area; yet even limited competence in cognate studies improves the quality of research by making available comparative data in history or literature from related regions or periods. In the end, a humanist should be in some measure a comparativist, whatever his particular discipline. The result would be that universities would find it possible to extend their cultural offerings at little expense.

Second, undergraduate programs could be expanded to make room, on a biennial or triennial basis, for courses taught for the non-specialist, in minority- and non-Western cultures. Such courses would not attract a significant number of students annually; but if they were scheduled so that every student had one chance in his undergraduate years to study a subject he had never heard about, they might attract enough students to justify their place in the curriculum.

Third, general-education courses in the social sciences and the humanities might include a greater variety of history and literature than they do at present. Having taught such courses, I realize that this may not seem to be a constructive suggestion. We teach far too much and too superficially. Yet if we were to teach by limited periods, over broader geographic regions, rather than by limited regions, over a broad span of time, we might find it practicable to include a greater variety of ethnic and cultural groups. The normal general-education course in the humanities, for example, includes important Western documents (among them those from non-Western regions which have become of importance to the West), from the Bible to the current novel. It might be equally practicable, given a sufficiently courageous staff, to teach ancient classics, adding to the writings of Israel, Greece, and Rome those of Assyria, Egypt, Iran, or Sumer; medieval classics, including those of Latin Christianity as well as some from the orthodox church; and, in addition, some particularly interesting writings selected from the literature of Islam, Hinduism, and medieval Judaism.

The same possibilities exist for history courses, though they would doubtless be equally difficult to develop. Medieval history, which deals with the history of the Middle Ages in Britain, France, Germany, and Italy, might usefully be broadened to include Islamic and Eastern European subjects. If Islam, in particular, is excluded from medieval history, one may seriously doubt whether the world as it was is truly being portrayed, for the Moslems did more than turn back the Crusades.

The fact is that men live in one world and always have; the various peoples of antiquity were far more closely interrelated than has been recognized even by sophisticated and literate persons; ideas passed freely from Greece and Israel to Iran and India and back again; moreover, the existential unity of mankind, particularly, but not only, in religious matters, requires that we have concern for everyone.

Some universities in the United States have specialized for many years in the language and culture of groups important in their particular constituencies. Scandinavian languages are not, to my knowledge, studied widely in the East or the Far West, but they are offered in the curriculums of universities in Wisconsin and Minnesota. Hebrew and Yiddish are taught in the City University of New York. Polish is offered in Milwaukee and Chicago. This practice springs from a serious desire to serve local constituencies realistically and usefully. It should be more extensively adopted by the universities and more actively supported by minority groups themselves. Too many institutions of higher education ignore large and interesting local ethnic groups and cultures. Every university should consider ways and means of presenting, in addition to the standard subjects, a program in a neglected foreign language or culture, so that eventually our universities, nationally as well as regionally, may justly lay claim to universal interests and a truly international perspective.

COMMENT

The case for ethnic studies needs to be weighed in the balance with the case against ethnic studies. Universities, however large, cannot cover all subjects for which one can make a case. Taste, judgment, and selection must limit the curriculum, if only because, by trying to do everything, we end up doing nothing well. But there is a further consideration. When we study a given literature or history, we must ask why, and especially we must explain for ourselves and our students the educational purpose we hope to attain. Simply to study this and that is no answer to the question, why are we learning these things? Merely to claim that there are people who want to learn them is unfair to those very people. For if all we have to offer is facts about one thing or another, what then are the meaning and logic of education? It is not, therefore, merely the practical problem of covering many cultures with a limited faculty which argues against the thesis of this paper. It is the more interesting question, Why are you telling me these things?

Our commitment in the humanities is to learning about humankind, and each theme or problem, history or language or literature, has to address itself to the question, What is it about the recorded experience of humankind which is learned distinctively and in a strikingly suggestive way in this literature or in this history? What do we wish to know about humankind? The particular and idiomatic must be asked to exemplify the general and universal. Obviously, that does not mean all that is important in the particular is what is to be learned about the generality of humankind. But there must, in

*a profound sense, be a common interest, an aspect of the common
human experience preserved in a given literature or related in a given
history, to which any curious person is able to relate, in which all of
us are able to find ourselves.*

*Further, in organizing the curriculum, it seems to me wisest to
group particular areas of study around common methods and disciplines, to foster mutual discourse among people who know different
things, but who know them in a common way. "Jewish studies" contain no discipline, though many disciplines illumine their data.
Established methods, to be learned in the study of any appropriate
datum, should open perspectives upon the new subjects of the curriculum, the ethnic studies in their several formulations. And, re-
ciprocally, the new data supplied by ethnic studies are going to test
the accepted methods and call into question their universal pertinence. For what we call "method" or "discipline" may in the encounter with new data prove to be little more than a rather specific
way of dealing with a single datum, a mode of generalizing about
what in fact is private. While the analytical modes of thought developed in Christian theology, for one example, may help in the
analysis of Jewish theology, nonetheless the closer one comes to the
data of Jewish theology—the actual writings of theologians—the
less obvious becomes the relevance of the "methods" of the Christian
theologians. The "discipline" turns out to be an exercise in the generalization of doctrine, not an enterprise in the detached analysis of
all religious ideas, deriving from any source whatever.*

*A further problem before ethnic studies is their incapacity to take
seriously the plural and diverse nature of the university, which ad-
mits whoever is qualified to learn, without regard to commitments of
faith, ethnic or racial origins, or other specificities. Shall we be content to see only Jewish students in courses on Judaism or Jewish
history, only black students in courses on the Afro-American experience? Shall we make the primary purpose of the course the improvement of an ethnic or racial self-image, the nurture of self-respect? It
seems to me that organizing departments of learning around the
several languages, histories, and cultures is apt to supply a mis-
leading signal about the nature and intent of such studies. At the*

same time, it is false to the nature of the groups themselves, people who, to be sure in idiomatic and distinctive ways, do share with all of humankind the same world, the same experiences of life, the same abiding human experiences and questions. If the Jews have something worth studying it is surely worth anyone's attention. We all bleed, we all suffer, we all die, we all have to explain to ourselves why. We should therefore be able to talk with one another.

II

JEWISH STUDIES IN THE UNIVERSITY

In *Reflections at Sixty,* Edmund Wilson published the suggestion, which both astonished and flattered Jewish scholars, that Judaism deserved study in his ideal university. He proposed that courses in the history and literature of the Jews be offered to both gentile and Jewish students, courses similar to those generally available in the histories of Greece and Rome, and in Greek and Latin literature in translation. Wilson wanted such courses to range beyond the commonplace "Old Testament" offerings, to include the literature of Judaism after the Maccabees. He cited such books as the apocryphal and Qumran writings, Josephus' *War* and *Antiquities,* the Talmud, Kabbala, Jewish law codes, and philosophy:

> The Jews should have at least as much place in our picture of civilization as they have had in our heritage of superstition. . . . These courses should be taught by a Jew. Few non-Jews would be competent to teach them. Jewish subjects have a way of becoming denatured when they pass through non-Jewish hands. Let the student be exposed to a Jewish scholar expounding without inhibition the traditions and the point of view of his own so-important people.

To evaluate Wilson's idea, one asks what is to be learned in Jewish studies. What place is there for such subjects in the world of discourse created by an American university?

If the continuing theme of the social sciences and humane letters is the nature of human experience, then Jewish studies will find a useful place in the university curriculum. They represent the effort to recover and record congeries of experiences almost unique in man's history, with few parallels and no precise duplicate. Apart from its intrinsic interest, Judaism, viewed dispassionately and analytically, provides an interesting example of the continuing interactions between ideas and men, religion and society, and history and culture.

The idea that animates Jewish history, the belief in an omnipotent, transcendent divine will, regulating the affairs of men and nations

18

and governing the movement of history, may have taken root only with difficulty and among only a few men in the First Jewish Commonwealth, before 586 B.C.E., but by the establishment of the Second Commonwealth it had begun to inform Jewish creativity and to provide a central theme for the national culture. The history of the growth of monotheism, its establishment among the Jews, and its development in response to challenges inherent both in its own dialectic and in its social settings, is not entirely clear. That this idea focused the continued development of Judaism is incontrovertible, however, and leads one to wonder: how did the Jews mediate between this idea and their own history? How did they persist in it through the several civilizations in which they participated? Why did their idea eventually conquer the West and much of the Orient as well, and why was its ultimate success achieved through the efforts of others? What further tasks in the development of the monotheist idea, after the end of biblical writing, remained for later generations, and how did men in successive new ages preserve the integrity of the original insight? In the history of the interaction between ideas and men the answers to these questions may well illumine broader areas of inquiry.

The central facts of Judaism have been the creation of a society founded on certain religious propositions, the translation of these propositions into operative law among some men, and the redefinition of the nation from that constituted by ethnic and territorial identity to that constituted by conviction and creed. If for the Christian the consequence of "revelation" has mostly yielded propositional faith, for the Jew it has yielded laws for the creation and governance of society. Hence the sociology of Judaism has a central place in its history. This sociology focused on two dominant themes, first, the conversion of nation to church during the Second Commonwealth, and second, the endurance of the nation-church afterward. There have been numerous exilic communities, such as the Parsees in India and the Overseas Chinese in southeast Asia, which offer significant parallels to the Jewish experience. What makes that experience unique has been the persistence of Jewish national aspiration throughout the history of the Diaspora, the aspiration not only to remain an identifiable cultural entity, but to return to rebuild the motherland. The Volga Germans, the Bombay Parsees, the Djakarta Chinese never aspired to go home, but the Jews did. One suspects that the development of the monotheist idea shaped the peculiar social destiny of Israel, and permitted the translation of her national images into universal, and in the Kabala even cosmic, symbols of historical redemption, without sacrificing their particular national implications. Perhaps the sociological consequences of unfulfilled messianic hopes are as significant as their theological implication; in any case, the Jews have suffered a very different history from the Parsees or the Overseas Chinese, and this history warrants study.

A third, lesser theme in the sociology of Judaism has been the translation of revelation into law, and the continued operation of such divinely-instituted law without the benefit of political institutions supported by state power. In the exilic political experience of Israel, Christians in particular may find useful lessons, for they too are beginning to experience spiritual and social "exile" in the aggressively secular cultures of both East and West. Human societies have manifested few such isolable and interesting examples of the interaction between religion and society, for if in the West religion yielded not law but philosophy and propositional faith, in the East it yielded not social or ethical obligation but psychological insight and infinite metaphysics.

The perplexity of history and culture embodied in American constitutionalism has rather complex parallels in Jewish cultural history. Judaism has always represented a commitment to Scripture, the "written constitution" of Israel, and has imposed on its adherents a fixed and sacred text. Jews obviously had to find a way to accommodate that text to extraordinarily varied conditions, at the same time preserving the integrity of a superficially rigid tradition and its contemporaneity. They mediated between the imperatives of history and the demands of existent culture through the medium of *midrash,* meaning, in its broader sense, the exegesis of sacred writ in the language and values of a later age. Judaism provides the classic paradigm of the tension between human freedom and authority. It explored a way toward constancy with the past in an inconstant world, and its experience ought to be relevant to men concerned with being both "modern" and truly Christian and Western.

These are areas of university discourse to which Judaism manifests some relevance. The university is not, of course, a formless conversation, but a highly structured world of discourse, with departments and courses of study. Within such a structure, Jewish studies might find a place in courses in the philosophy of religion (most such studies in this country would be more accurately labeled the philosophy of Protestant Christianity and its heretics, Catholic antecedents being retroactively converted, or ignored); in the sociology of religion, particularly in studies on types of religious communities; in the social and economic history of the West, for the treatment of the Jews has frequently been symptomatic of the condition of the host-culture; in the history of mysticism; in the psychology of religion—Judaism has its unique types of religious leadership and religious experience; and in comparative literature of the ancient, medieval, and modern periods. Offerings in Jewish studies, however multi-disciplinary the approach, need to find a place in specific departments such as these. At present scholars of Jewish studies teach in a variety of departments—in some places in the Semitics Department, whose main interests are in classical Semitic philology and, to a lesser extent, in the Hebrew Bible, and normally not in the post-Biblical history of the Jews; in other places in history, comparative literature, philosophy, or sociology departments. Where there is a Department of Religion, Jewish studies provide a useful extension of departmental interests. At one university, "Hebraic Civilization" is part of the offering of the Department of Classical Languages, at another, of modern languages.

It is crucial, however, to preserve the essentially inter-disciplinary character of Jewish studies. Ideally such studies, reduced to the limits of a course-offering, ought to be conceived within the framework of general education, rather than as specialized and limited additions to departmental offerings in history, sociology, or philosophy. Two types of courses might be congruent to the general-education approach, a "Jewish humanities" and a "Jewish social sciences" (or, as it is called at Columbia, a Jewish "contemporary civilization" course). The pedagogical problem to be solved by Jewish scholars is to reduce the complex disciplines of Jewish learning to a simple sequence and order. Judaism cannot be reduced to a geometry, of course, but it needs to be reduced to a history, or, more specifically, to a history-of-ideas or a history-of-literature or "philosophy" course. Approaching the history of Judaism one finds order and development only with great difficulty because there has never been such a thing as "Judaism," but rather "Judaisms," the Judaism of the mystics, of the rationalists, of the lawyers, of the moralists, of the poets, of the codifiers, of the scientific scholars, of the nationalists—and even of the municipal authorities. All these constitute expressions of Judaism, and all offer significant insights. The continuities of Jewish faith and culture emerge from study of their complexities; to reduce "Judaisms" to the "essentials of Judaism" yields something neither authentic nor even recognizable. Yet to preserve the integrity of every kind of Judaism within the boundaries of a single course produces confusion.

I should suggest that a course in the history of Judaism might contain the following sequences of study: first, the Hebrew Scriptures from the perspective of Judaism, that is, the history not of "Old Testament Witness," but of monotheism from its earliest social and theological manifestations to the Maccabees; second, the history of the Second Commonwealth, from the Maccabees to the end of the Mishnah and Talmud, following (because of its later normative character) the main lines of Pharisaism, and Rabbinic-Talmudic Judaism, with excursions into Hellenistic Judaism, early Judeo-Christianity, Gnosticism, and Zoroastrianism, with emphasis on midrashic and Talmudic literature; third, the history of the exilic community from the Arab conquest to the European emancipation, in two parts, first, Judaism under Islam, including the history of Jewish rationalist philosophy, medieval literature, theology, and poetry; and second, the history of Judaism under Christendom, including the after-life of the Talmud and its study, legal codes, the constitution of the self-contained, autonomous exilic community and its social institutions, medieval anti-semitism, the rise of Kabbalah, Hassidism, Sabbateanism (this ought to be of special interest to Christian historians, for the history of the early Church finds significant parallels in Sabbateanism); and finally, the history of Judaism in the modern world (since 1800), including the tardy Enlightenment, Science [Wissenschaft], and reformation of Judaism, the response of traditionalism, in the East through the ethical movement, in the West through "orthodoxy," and Jewish national, intellectual, and cultural rebirth in eastern and western Europe and Israel, the Jewish experience in America, and Judaism after the experience of radical evil during World War II. These sequences provide insight into the various religious and cultural movements, even though some of them are overlapping (Islam and Christendom) or even unrelated. The point of such a course ought to be to introduce the literature and thought of Israel through the ages and to help the student read and understand some of the authentic, classic texts of Judaism (in English translation) and their central concerns and images. The student might well find for himself the elements of continuing concern that lie behind the notion of a unitary "Judaism" in such continuities and recurrent images, and in the varieties of their use. The range and discourse ought always to be as broad as possible, with reference to parallel historical and cultural events.

Such studies ought to lead eventually to a more precise definition of the so-called Judeo-Christian tradition that is supposed to provide fundamental wisdom for American civilization. The "Judeo-" part of that tradition has been mostly Hebrew Scriptures, read through Christian spectacles. However, the Jews, as well as their Scriptures, have played some part in the history of most Western nations at some time. For the most part, this role has been, as Wilson pointed out, to provide evil visions and dark images. The Jews have had a far more central role in the creation of modernism than has been generally noted. Marx, Freud, and Einstein were not only Jews, but enormously self-consciously so. One can hardly find all the sources of their respective metaphysics outside the collapsing walls of the nineteenth-century ghetto. In the exploration of the Judeo-Christian tradition that lies behind American culture, men might well want to explore specifically the Jewish background of modernism.

If Hitler had had complete instead of partial success, there would probably be deep interest in the history and literature of an ancient, tragic people. No doubt there is greater academic respectability in the exhumation of the dead than in the examination of the living. The Jews are, however, present in America and in the world. They have produced records of a social experience, a fundamental idea, a complex culture, that will probably reward serious study. There are, moreover, some men, Jewish and gentile, who want to address themselves to the problems discussed in universities, and to offer the modest wisdom suggested by their own particular knowledge of the Jewish records. I do not agree with Wilson that such men themselves must be confessing Jews; such a criterion would exclude such Christian scholars as George F. Moore and Herbert Danby, as well as other scholars of Jewish birth but not of formal commitment to the Jewish faith. Judaism needs no special pleading, and in any case any effort at indoctrination would violate the canons of intellectual freedom and university discourse. The interest of most students of Judaism is not confessional. The criteria ought to be technical, including linguistic competence, sympathy, and understanding. If most students of Judaism are Jews, their purpose in the university is nonetheless to illumine, where they can, a continuing conversation, if only by suggesting a different perspective.

One recalls in this connection Yvor Winters' "Ode on the Despoilers of Learning in an American University":

> This was our heritage:
> In learning's monument
> To study and teach the young
> Until our days were spent;
> To reembody mind
> In age succeeding age,
> That some few men might see,
> Though mostly men were blind;
> To hold what men had wrung
> From struggle to atone
> For man's stupidity,
> In labor, and alone.

If the Jews have had some insight, that vision ought to be shared in the places where men's eyes are still open.

COMMENT

Here are answers to the question, to what larger problems and themes of university discourse does the study of Judaism relate? These are the wrong answers. Indeed, it would be difficult to propose a surer recipe for superficiality, excessive generalization, and mealy-mouthed platitudes, than is contained in this paper. The conception that the study of Judaism should proceed along inter-disciplinary lines is blindly to miss the point of the study of Judaism. It is to claim that all that is of interest is found at the points at which Judaism is able to illuminate matters of common concern, problems important elsewhere, defined in other settings, with no regard whatever for the particular morphology of Judaism itself.

The underlying error is in the angle of approach. Do we start with the issues common to university discourse, then construct an apologia for the study of Judaism based upon its pertinence to those issues? That is what is at the foundation of this paper, which claims too little and apologizes too much. It is true that Judaism provides an interesting example of the continuing interactions between ideas and men, religion and society, and history and culture. But (bypassing the high-falutin' categories) is what is authentic to and important in the study of Judaism the issue of the interplay between religion and society? Is this what we are supposed to learn? I think quite to the contrary that these issues (properly defined, not in platitudes) illuminate the study of Judaism and are important because they help us to understand its phenomena. This is for two reasons.

First, quite bluntly, no area studied in university curriculums is evaluated in such terms, so why Judaism (or black studies, or Polish studies)? These rigorous demands, coupled with stratospheric claims, come from outsiders. I doubt that scholars in the established fields, for instance, Classics or French literature or American history, commonly ask themselves how they advance the inquiry into the larger issues of the relationship between "history and culture." I wonder whether even once a year professors of English literature ask themselves what they might understand by "culture."

Second, if anything worthwhile, more than vapid generalization,

*ever is learned and remembered, it is mastered in the details of a
subject. We build with very tiny blocks. We understand beginning
with ourselves, with our capacity to transform what we learn about
the world into something we can relate to our own insight and our
own problem. Accordingly, when we necessarily seek for what
speaks to everyone, we must listen to Jews speaking in the most concrete and intimate voices, among themselves. Then, without self-
consciousness and posturing, they talk about what is private and
idiomatic, which therefore is universal and human. For at home, by
themselves, they ask, What is the way in which a man should walk
in order to find life in the world to come?—a man (or a woman) and
not a Jew. The language of the classics of Judaism is peculiar, but
it also is unself-conscious and therefore accessible. It needs to be
allowed to find its corresponding words in the languages of others.
The arcane must be shown to be lucid. The particular must be
shown to speak about humankind. But this can be done only in the
details, in the very specificities of the documents themselves which
contain whatever aspects of Judaism can be examined in a university.*

*Rather than blather about religion and society, I should rather
read Mishnah and Talmud, documents which, in their ineluctable
indifference to generalizations, are meant to relate religion to society
and obliterate the distinctions between them. Rather than speak
about "history and culture," I should study the theoretical literature
of Zionism and the development of modern Hebrew literature, and
study these in detail and with care, so that, in the remarkable creation of a new culture in response to massive historical events, Judaism may be allowed to show what is at issue.*

*I still am moved by Winters' ode, "To reembody mind in age suc-
ceeding age," yes—that is the point. But to reembody mind, we
have to confront the works of minds, the things people actually do,
make, and think, the concrete vision about some specific place and
time. It is indeed a struggle to gain vision. But to share a vision,
we must enter into the being of a real man or woman; not talk about
the prophets, but read their words; not "analyze and discuss" the
priestly conception of the world, but read Genesis and Leviticus. In*

the author's defense, it should be pointed out that he was young and did not know very much. He still may not know a whole lot, but he is no longer young. He lives "to study and teach the young until our days were spent," because, in his time and in his place, he is the one who bears primary responsibility for that work. Elsewhere or in other days, it is and will be the task of others. But now and here, it is his—a humbling fact.

Part Two

THE THEOLOGICAL STUDY
OF JUDAISM

THE THEOLOGICAL STUDY OF JUDAISM

Introduction

In order to understand what is, or should be, new in the academic setting for Jewish learning and, in particular, for the study of Judaism, we have to spell out the modes of thought characteristic of Jewish settings for Jewish learning. This is in two parts. First, we consider what the act of learning meant in the classical context of belief. The fact that, in Judaism, studying is itself sacred bears curious implications for the study of Judaism in universities and imposes an ineluctable tension. These implications become clear when we consider the characteristics of Jewish scholarship in the nineteenth and twentieth centuries, from the founding of the Science of Judaism *(Wissenschaft des Judenthums)*.

This new and interesting mode of Jewish learning found itself in an ambiguous and unwelcome situation. On the one hand, the creators of the Science of Judaism were trained in universities—chiefly in philosophy, philology, and history—and absorbed the values of their masters. On the other, those few who to begin with were gainfully employed as scholars were located in Jewish theological institutions. While, therefore, modern academic modes of scholarship were readily absorbed into the world of Jewish learning, and nineteenth- and twentieth-century academic values were assimilated, scholars of Judaism recognized a conflict between their work, as teachers of rabbis or as communal rabbis, and their values as scholars. In the present era a response to this conflict is in the insistence, upon the part of teachers in theological seminaries, that they are truly objective and advocate nothing more than mere facts. This clashes with the troubled and doubting contention of scholars of

31

Judaism in universities that the meaning of objectivity is not wholly clear, the nature and facticity of facts not yet established.

The second of the two papers attempts to delineate the scholarly continuities of classical propositions of faith, presented in the name of history and under the guise of objective scholarship, and asks whether scholarship has not paid a heavy price for its incapacity—because scholars to begin with said they had no values at all—to achieve self-consciousness. For it is only the true believer who believes nothing by faith, because what he believes is only what he knows, is merely factual.

These two papers, like the first two of the next section, are meant to illustrate the ambiguity of the issue in its current formulation, what is the task of the scholar *vis à vis* the tradition. On the one side, it is argued that the scholar, in doing what he does, embodies an important ideal of the tradition (if only partially). On the other, it is alleged that the scholar who claims to be detached, uncommitted, and objective in respect of the tradition thereby prevents himself or herself from truly understanding what, in his or her scholarly results, may have been shaped within the tradition itself.

The first of the two papers is in no way meant to be polemical. The second, obviously, is highly polemical. Perhaps the polemic may obscure the argument, which is to be regretted. But so far as the academic study of Judaism thus far has created an arena for scholarly discourse, arguments tend to be polemical. That is hardly inappropriate to the subject, for the real issues are immediate and profound, the definition of Judaism, the delimiting of the nature and meaning of Jewishness, the description of the appropriate roles open to Jewish intellectuals and scholars. That is, it is not possible to avoid classical theological issues, and theology evidently generates a measure of polemic, while scholarship does not. When, to put matters more simply, we touch deeply held convictions and challenge their facticity and givenness, as we do, it is inevitable that polemic will result. So why not at the outset?

III

CLASSICAL JUDAISM AND THE INTELLECT

Let us begin by defining "classical" or "Rabbinic" Judaism. It is commonly, and wrongly, supposed that "Judaism" is equivalent to the so-called "Old Testament," and that "what the Jews believe" is summarized therein. For example, speaking of Henry Kissinger, then Vice President Ford said, "He is of the faith of the Old Testament." Two common mistakes are contained in that commonplace description of the Jews' religion. First, it is taken for granted that the Jews call the biblical books from Genesis to Malachi "the Old Testament." Second, it is imagined that the Jewish religion may be located and defined solely and entirely by opening the pages of "the Old Testament."

Now what difference does it make that what Christians call "Old Testament" has a different name for Judaism?

The difference is important. When Christians say "Old Testament," it is because they believe there is a "New Testament," which completes and fulfills the old. They see the religion of ancient Israel as insufficient, referring as it does to a Messiah who, by the end of the story, still has not yet come. More importantly, they understand in the life and teachings of Jesus the fulfillment of the "Old Testament" prophecies. In other words, Christianity in nearly all its forms takes over the Hebrew Scriptures and supplies them with a vast interpretation based upon the life and teachings of Jesus, whom they call Christ, or messiah. Everyone knows this.

What is not widely known is that, from the first century onward, Judaism took the same view of the Hebrew Scriptures. It concurred in the view that the ancient writings of Israel contained in the Tanakh

33

presented only part of the story. The other part, Judaism held, was contained in the other Torah—in addition to the written Torah revealed in ancient times—taught in their own day by rabbis. We shall come back to this matter in a moment. The main point is that Judaism and Christianity agree on the sanctity of the *Old Testament* = *Tanakh,* but disagree about its meaning.

Judaism is based upon both the written Torah and a second Torah, just as Christianity is based upon the Old Testament and a second and a new "Testament" or covenant. Where do we now find this second Torah, this other (and, as we shall see, *oral*) revelation? It is found in the Mishnah, a corpus of traditions and laws written down at the end of the second century C.E. ("Common Era," sometimes used by Jews in place of A.D., because of the theological significance of A.D.—Anno Domini, the year of the Lord).

For the present, we may therefore summarize with the following equation:

$$\text{Christianity} \qquad\qquad \text{Judaism}$$

$$\frac{Old\ Testament}{\text{New Testament}} \quad = \quad \frac{Tanakh}{\text{Mishnah}}$$

What a curious equation! The parts are unequal. Everyone has heard of Old Testament and New Testament. Everyone knows how the New Testament writers, for example, in the Gospel of Matthew, will cite the Old Testament as predicting events in the life of Jesus. But the words of the Judaic side of the equation are alien and strange. Few have heard of *Tanakh,* and very few of *Mishnah.*

That is why we begin with the observation that to describe a Jew as "of the faith of the Old Testament" is simply inaccurate. But it is meant to stress something else. Judaism is not simply the religion of people who do not believe that Jesus is the messiah. It also is not the sum and substance of the opinions of everyone who is Jewish, to be decided by a public opinion poll of all such people. It is not something we know about automatically, just as we naturally know a great deal about Christianity, its festivals, religious rites and beliefs, simply by going to public school or by studying Western civilization, or watching television, going to the movies, and the like. Judaism is a religion which is present (if not in equivalently vast numbers), just as Christianity is present, in the Western world. Yet ·it is one of the world's least known religions. And part of the reason is that most people think they know something about it, when, in fact, they know very little, and what they know is at best half-true.

Much that follows is going to be alien not only to Christians and people of no religious origin but also to Jews. That makes our problem still more difficult. Commonly, Jews know about Judaism only what is to be gained in a smattering of Sunday School lessons or in half-remembered sermons heard on the few occasions which found them in Jewish worship. What makes this an obstacle is their sense of "having heard it all," when, in fact, they have understood very little. Many of the words they have heard or said in prayer, for example, have not attracted their close attention. Some of the things we shall consider will seem familiar, while what we shall say about them appears to be strange. If we can commence with the agreement that we are studying a strange and alien religion, that everything we shall hear is new and fresh, we can build an accurate description of Judaism.

Let us now turn to the central and distinctive mode of religious experience in classical or Rabbinic Judaism, its stress upon learning as a religious experience, its conviction that when we use our minds, we serve God. This is an alien and remote conception, even though most Jews know the commonplace that "the study of Torah outweighs all the rest," and realize that their religion lays great emphasis upon learning. This conception will be seriously misinterpreted if we suppose that what Judaism wants is for everyone to get a Ph.D., or for everyone to engage in the learned professions, for instance, law or medicine. That is why I stressed that we have to approach Judaism as if we know nothing about it, as if we are anthropologists coming to a strange, alien tribe in New Guinea or the Amazon. Then we can hear words for the first time and ask about their meaning in their own context.

For nearly twenty centuries the central and predominant commitment of Rabbinic Judaism, that is, that form of Judaism deemed normative and generative of the Judaic understanding of existence, has been to learning, and, specifically, to what is called "study of Torah." "Study of Torah" is understood in a very specific way, as devotion to the learning both of the Scriptures, held to be the written revelation of God to Moses at Sinai, and of the *Torah shebe'al peh*, the Oral revelation, concommitant with the written one. "The whole Torah of Moses"—oral and written—constituted the sum and substance of Rabbinic Judaism, its claim upon legitimacy and spiritual hegemony in Israel. The history of Judaism, therefore, is primarily the work of men who believed that at the center of the religious life lies the act of learning, at the focus of the experience of the sacred is the activity of the mind.

In the literature of Rabbinic Judaism we find numerous sayings to express this most fundamental conviction, for instance, "Piety without learning in Torah is impossible." "Study of Torah outweighs all else." It goes without saying that Rabbinism furthermore maintained everyone is to become learned and, in its healthiest moments, made provision for all classes of male Israelites to join the Rabbinic estate, to study and master Torah. My purpose is to analyze this mode of religious expression and to explain what is, or can be, religious about learning.

Let me first distinguish Rabbinic intellectualism from Western scholarship. To the rabbi, the question of Tertullian, "What has Athens to do with Jerusalem, the Academy with the Church," has no meaning. He could not have grasped a distinction between the piety of the synagogue and the activity of the academy, the *yeshivah*. The one was the pale reflection of the other. Since, as I shall stress, God is not only revealer of the Torah, but also studies in a heavenly academy, what man does below is a reflection of the true reality above. To ask what learning has to do with piety, one to begin with would have to conceive God other than as master of Torah and the imitation of God other than as learning. Such a conception lies wholly outside the rabbinic framework. The rabbi likewise cannot grasp the question, What is the use of it all? For to him, the answer is too obvious to legitimate the question. Perceiving no distinction between intellect and soul or spirit, he cannot wonder about the relationship between learning and devotion, between mind and spirit. If he is a mystic—and many have been—he composes a book on mystical doctrine, not merely experiencing mystical reality. If he is a philosopher, his philosophy becomes a mode of Torah. If he is a lawyer, the mastery of the law is the highest expression of his piety; the study of details of the law is holy in itself.

Clearly, this total integration of faith and intellect, both at its most fundamental level and in its most superficial effects, is the result of the apprehension of a profoundly mythic conception of life, of the perfect correspondence between myth and the reality both shaped and interpreted by myth. Let me therefore turn to the Torah-myth of Rabbinic Judaism and explain its substance.

The encompassing myth revealed of Rabbinic Judaism centers upon the figure of Moses and tells the story of the Moses-piety—spirituality centered on Moses—of the rabbis. That story relates God's disclosure to Moses of a dual revelation, or Torah, at Mount Sinai—one in writing, the other handed orally from master to disciple. The whole Torah—oral and written—contains the design for the universe, the divine architect's plan for reality. It is to be studied, therefore, not merely for information, but as an act of piety and reverence for the divine lawgiver. Just as God teaches Torah to Moses, so the rabbi, modeling his life after Moses "our rabbi," teaches his own disciple. In "studying Torah," and even more so in effecting it in the lives of Israel, the rabbi thus imitates God. Following the model of the "school" in heaven, the schools for Torah-study bring together masters and disciples and preserve the ancient traditions.

The most striking aspect of these schools is the rabbis' conception that in them live holy men, men who more accurately than anyone else conform to the image of God conveyed by divine revelation through the Torah of Moses "our rabbi." The schools are not holy places only or primarily in the sense that pious people make pilgrimages to them or that miracles are supposed to take place there. The schools are holy because there men achieve sainthood through study of Torah and imitation of the conduct of the masters. In doing so, they conform to the heavenly paradigm, the Torah, believed to have been created by God "in his image," revealed at Sinai, and handed down to their own teachers. Thus obedience to the teachings of the rabbis leads not merely to ethical or moral goodness, but to holiness or sainthood. Discussion of legal traditions, rather than ascetic disciplines or long periods of fasting and prayer, is the rabbis' way to holiness.

If the masters and disciples obey the divine teaching of Moses our rabbi, then their society, the school, replicates on earth the heavenly academy, just as the disciple incarnates the heavenly model of Moses our rabbi. The rabbis believe that Moses is a rabbi, God dons phylacteries, and the heavenly court studies Torah precisely as does the earthly one, even arguing about the same questions. These beliefs today may be seen as projections of rabbinical values onto heaven, but the rabbis believe that they themselves are projections of heavenly values onto earth. The rabbis thus conceive that on earth they study Torah just as God, the angels, and Moses our rabbi do in heaven. The heavenly schoolmen are even aware of scholastic discussions, so they require a rabbi's information about an aspect of purity-taboos.

So the rabbis believe that the man truly made in the divine image is the rabbi; he embodies revelation—both oral and written—and all his actions constitute paradigms that are not merely correct, but holy and heavenly. Rabbis enjoy exceptional grace from heaven. Torah is held to be a source of supernatural power. The rabbis control the power of Torah because of their mastery of its contents. They furthermore use their own mastery of Torah quite independent of heavenly action. They issue blessings and curses, create men and animals, and master witchcraft, incantations, and amulets. They communicate with heaven. Their Torah is sufficiently effective to thwart the action of demons. However much they disapprove of other people's magic, they themselves do the things magicians do.

The rabbis furthermore want to transform the entire Jewish community into an academy where the whole Torah was studied and kept. This belief aids in understanding the rabbis' view that Israel will be redeemed through Torah. Because Israel had sinned, it was punished by being given over into the hands of earthly empires;

when it atones, it will be removed from their power. The means of this atonement or reconciliation are study of Torah, practice of commandments, and doing good deeds. These transform each Jew into a rabbi, hence into a saint. When all Jews become rabbis, they then will no longer lie within the power of history. The Messiah will come. So redemption depends upon the "rabbinization" of all Israel, that is, upon the attainment by all Jewry of a full and complete embodiment of revelation or Torah, thus achieving a perfect replica of heaven. When Israel on earth becomes such a replica, it will be able, as a righteous, and saintly community, to exercise the supernatural power of Torah, just as some rabbis are already doing. With access to the consequent theurgical capacities, redemption will naturally follow. The issues of Rabbinic analysis, while rationally investigated, thus are transcendent and cosmic in significance.

If in other religious traditions holiness is expressed through ascetic, flesh-suppressing disciplines—through sitting on pillars or dwelling in caves, through eating only wormwood and dressing only in rags, the rabbis' sainthood consists in the analysis of trivial and commonplace things through practical and penetrating logic and criticism. Their chief rite is *argument*. To be sure, they pray like other people, but to them, learning in Torah is peculiarly "ours," praying is "theirs" —that of ordinary folk. Their heroes are men of learning, and they turned their biblical heroes, beginning with Moses, into men of learning.

The rabbis conceive of practical and critical thinking as holy, claim sainthood in behalf of learned men, see as religiously significant, indeed as sanctified, what the modern intellectual perceives as the very instrument of secularity: the capacity to think critically and to reason. Here is the mystery of Rabbinic Judaism: the (to us) alien and remote conviction that the intellect is an instrument not of unbelief and desacralization but of sanctification. That conviction is the most difficult aspect of Rabbinism to comprehend, because it is so easy to misunderstand and misrepresent. The external form of the belief—our ability to think clearly, to be mindful—is readily accessible to us. But the meaning of the belief, its substance, its place in the shaping of the religious imagination and the formation of the religious and traditional culture of the Jewish people—these are not so obvious.

To grasp the meaning of Rabbinic intellectualism, therefore, we have to turn to its substance, its conception of the world, man, and God. The presupposition of the Rabbinic approach to life is that order is better than chaos, reflection than whim, decision than accident, ratiocination and rationality than witlessness and force. The only admissible force is the power of fine logic, ever refined against the gross matter of daily living. The sole purpose is so to construct the discipline of everyday life and to pattern the relationships among men that all things are intelligible, well-regulated, trustworthy,—and sanctified. Rabbinic Judaism stands for the perfect intellectualization of life, that is, the subjection of life to rational study. For nothing is so trivial as to be unrelated to some conceptual, abstract principle. If the placing of a napkin or the washing of the hands is subject to critical analysis, what can be remote from rigorous inquiry? But the mode of inquiry is not man's alone. Man is made in God's image. And that part of man which is like God is not corporeal. It is the thing which separates man from beast: the mind, consciousness. When man uses his mind, he is acting like God. That surely is a conviction uncharacteristic of modern intellectuals, yet at the heart of Rabbinic intellectuality.

Rabbinic Judaism single-mindedly pursues unifying truths. But that search does not derive from the perception of unifying order in the natural world. It comes, rather, from the lessons imparted supernaturally in the Torah. The sages perceive the Torah not as a mélange of sources and laws of different origins, but as a single, unitary document, a corpus of laws reflective of an underlying ordered will. The Torah reveals the way things should be, just as the rabbis' formulation and presentation of their laws tell how things should be, whether or not that is how they actually are done. The order derives from the plan and will of the Creator of the World, the foundation of all reality. The Torah is interpreted by the rabbis to be the architect's design for reality: God looked into the Torah and created the world, just as an architect follows his prior design in raising a building. A single, whole Torah—in two forms, oral and written, to be sure—underlies the one, seamless reality of the world. The search for the unities hidden by the pluralities of the trivial world, the supposition that some one thing is revealed by many things—these represent in intellectual form the theological and metaphysical conception of a single, unique God, creator of heaven and earth, revealer of one complete Torah, guarantor of the unity and ultimate meaning of all the human actions and events that constitute history. On that account Rabbinism links the private deeds of man to a larger pattern, provides a large and general 'meaning' for small, particular, trivial doings.

Behind this conception of the unifying role of reason and of law and the integrating force of practical criticism of everyday behavior lies the conviction that God supplies the model for man's mind, therefore man, through reasoning in the Torah's laws, may penetrate into God's intent and plan. The rabbis believe they study Torah as God does in heaven; their schools are conducted like the academy on high. They perform rites just as God performed rites, wearing fringes as He does, putting on phylacteries just as God put on phylacteries. In studying Torah, they seek to conform to the heavenly paradigm, revealed by God "in his image" and handed down from Moses and the prophets to their own teachers. If the rabbis study and realize the divine teaching of Moses, whom they call "our rabbi," it is because the order they impose upon earthly affairs replicates on earth the order they perceive from heaven, the rational construction of reality. It is Torah which reveals the mind of God, the principles by which he shapes reality. So studying Torah is not merely imitating God, who does the same, but is a way to apprehension of God and the attainment of the sacred. The modes of argument are holy because they lead from earth to heaven, as prayer or fasting or self-denial cannot. Reason is God's way, and the holy man is therefore he who is able to think clearly and penetrate profoundly into the mysteries of the Torah and, especially, of its so very trivial laws. In context, those trivialities contain revelation.

What is distinctively Rabbinic is perpetual skepticism, expressed in response to every declarative sentence or affirmative statement. Once one states that matters are so, it is inevitable that he will find as a response: Why do you think so? Or, perhaps things are the opposite of what you say? Or, how can you say so when a contrary principle may be adduced? Articulation, forthrightness, subtle reasoning but lucid expression, skepticism—these are the traits of intellectuals, not of untrained and undeveloped minds, nor of scholars, capable only to serve as curators of the past, but not as critics of the present.

Above all, Rabbinic thinking rejects gullibility and credulity. It is, indeed, peculiarly modern in its systematic skepticism, its testing of each proposition, not to destroy but to refine what people suppose to be so. The Talmud's first question is not "Who says so," but, "Why?" "What is the reason of the House of Shammai?" In the Rabbinic approach to thought, faith is restricted to ultimate matters, to the fundamental principles of reality beyond which one may not penetrate.

Let us dwell on the centrality of skepticism in the Rabbinic mode of thinking. Virtually as soon as the primary document of the Oral Torah, the Mishnah, or law-code of Judah the Patriarch, reached its present form at the beginning of the third century A.D., the process of criticism and skeptical inquiry began. The people who received the oral tradition, the Amoraim, engaged in a far-reaching search for imperfections in the Mishnah, in the certainty of its ultimate perfection. It must have taken considerable courage to criticize an authoritative law-code, the Mishnah, and its accompanying supplement, the Tosefta. It would have been pious merely to accept those laws and digest them for future generations to memorize and copy. Judah the Patriarch, called "our holy rabbi," and those whose traditions he organized and handed on were very ancient authorities. Two or three centuries later, the prestige of the Mishnah, regarded, as we saw, as the "Oral Torah" revealed by Moses at Sinai, was considerable. To ask for reasons, to criticize those reasons, to seek contradictions, to add to the law, to revise or even reject what the ancients had said—these are acts of men who have or lay no equivalent claim either to first-hand knowledge of the Oral Torah or to the sanctity and prestige of the Tannaim. Yet that is exactly what the Amoraim did. And they did so in such a way as to revise everything that had gone before, to place upon the whole heritage of the past the indelible and distinct, unmistakable stamp of their own minds.

The reason is that the Amoraim did not confuse respect with servility. They carefully nurtured the disciples' critical and creative faculties. Gibbon said (probably unfairly) of the Byzantine schools, "Not a single composition of history, philosophy, or literature has been saved from oblivion by the intrinsic beauties of style, or sentiment, or original fancy, or even of successful imitation." By contrast, the Talmud and later Rabbinic writings are the product not of servility to the past or of dogmatism in the present, but of an exceptionally critical, autonomous rationalism and an utterly independent spirit. The Amoraim and later authorities gave to pedantry a cool welcome. Clearly, to them mere learning is insufficient. Not what one knows, but what he can do with what he knows, is decisive. The authority and approbation of the elders are set aside by the critical accomplishments of the newest generation. In the fullest sense, the Amoraim and their heirs are not traditionalists. They take the laws and traditions of the early generations into their care, respectfully learning them, reverently handing them on. But these they thoroughly digest and make their own. Their minds are filled with the learning of the ancients. But their rational wisdom and unrelenting criticism are wholly their own.

The Rabbinic stress upon criticism produces a new freedom of construction, the freedom to reinterpret reality and to reconstruct its artifacts upon the basis of well-analyzed, thoroughly criticized principles revealed through the practical reason of the sages. Once a person is free to stand apart from what is customary and habitual, to restrain energies and regulate them, he attains the higher freedom to revise the given, to reinterpret established perceptions of reality and the institutions which give them effect. This constitutes, to begin with, the process of the mind's focusing upon unseen relationships and the formation of imposed, non-material and non-natural considerations. We recall in this connection the purity laws, which play so considerable a role in the rabbis' regulation of eating (and other fundamental things, for instance, sexual relations). Those laws seem to have comprised and created a wholly abstract set of relationships, a kind of non-Euclidean geometry of the levitical realm. Yet those high abstractions are brought down to earth to determine in what order one washes his hands and picks of a cup of wine or where one puts his napkin. So what is wholly relative and entirely a matter of theory, not attached to concrete things, transforms trivialities. It affects, indeed generates, the way one does them. It transforms them to the higher meanings (to be sure, without much rational, let alone material substance) associated with the pure and the impure. The purity laws stand at the pinnacle of Rabbinic abstraction and ratiocination.

Rabbinic criticism is in four modes: (1) abstract, rational criticism of each tradition in sequence and of the answers hazarded to the several questions; (2) historical criticism of sources and their (un)harmonious relationship; (3) philological and literary criticism of the meanings of words and phrases; and (4) practical criticism of what people actually do in order to carry out their religious obligations. It goes without saying that these four modes of criticism are peculiarly contemporary. Careful, skeptical examination of answers posed to problems is utterly commonplace to modern men and women. Historical criticism of sources, which does not gullibly accept whatever is alleged as fact, is the beginning of historical study. Philological study of the origins and meanings of words, literary criticism of the style of expression—these are familiar. Finally, we take for granted that it is normal to examine peoples' actions against some large principle of behavior. These are traits of inquiry which are both Talmudic and routinely modern.

What makes them different from modern modes of thought? It is the remarkable claim that in the give and take of argument, in the processes of criticism, one does something transcendent, more than this-worldly. I cannot overemphasize how remarkable is the combination of rational criticism and supernatural value attached to that criticism. We simply cannot understand Rabbinic Judaism without confronting the other-worldly context in which this so completely secular thinking goes forward. The claim is that in seeking reason and order, you serve God. But what are we to make of that claim?

Does lucid thinking bring heavenly illumination? How can people suggest so?

Perhaps the best answer may be sought in this-worldly experience. Whence comes insight? Having put everything together in a logical and orderly way, we sometimes find ourselves immobilized. We know something, but we do not know what it means, what it suggests beyond itself. Then, sometimes, we catch an unexpected insight, and come in some mysterious way to a comprehension of a whole which exceeds the sum of its parts. And we cannot explain how we have seen what, in a single instant, stuns us by its ineluctable rightness, fittingness—by the unearned insight, the inexplicable understanding. For the rabbis that stunning moment of rational insight comes with *siyyata dishamaya,* the help of heaven. The charisma imparted by the Rabbinic imagination to the brilliant man is not different in substance from the moral authority and spiritual dignity imparted by contemporary intellectuals to the great minds of the age. The profound honor to be paid to the intellectual paragons —the explorers of the unknown, the men and women of courage to doubt the accepted truths of the hour—is not much different from the deference shown by the disciple to the rabbi. So the religious experience of the rabbi and the secular experience of the intellectual differ not in quality. They gravely differ in the ways by which we explain and account for that experience. Still, in reflecting upon the commonalities of experience, we are enabled to enter into the curious mode of religiosity discovered within the Talmud.

Rabbinic Judaism divorced from its mythic context, its larger meanings for the construction of reality and the interpretation of life, is nothing else than a mere tradition. And a tradition perceived as traditional is also conceived as passed. But the Talmud, the central document of Rabbinic Judaism, understood as an expression of religion, as the statement of the inner world of saints, becomes a vivid alternative. For ultimate meanings are not bound to a particular place or time, and a way to the sacred, once discovered, remains forever open. What today is sought, and I think what is acutely required, is not what we already have, but what we realize we do not have: a mythic context for our being, a larger world of meanings for our private and individual existence. These have been found by seekers of mystic experience in the suppression of the intellect and the willful suspension of unbelief. With the Talmud we are able to see them in the cultivation of the intellect and the criticism even of belief. The mystery of the Talmud and of the Judaism founded on it is its capacity to sanctify the one thing we do not propose to abandon, which is our capacity to doubt, our commitment to criticize, above all, the beautiful, reasoned, open-ended discourse created among contentions, learning men and women. The wonder of the Talmud is its tough-minded claims in behalf of the intellect as a mode of the sacred.

COMMENT

This paper underlines the peculiar ambiguity of the academic study of sacred texts by people who derive from the community to which those texts are or were sacred. If we study Tanakh or Mishnah or Maimonides in the university class-room, we in fact engage in an act which, from the perspective of Judaism, is religious. However detached and objective we may prove to be, however carefully we distinguish between the text and ourselves, the text testifies against us. For when we learn in Avot *that we were made to study Torah, and read the texts which in Judaism constitute Torah, whether we like it or not, we therefore are understood by those texts to be doing precisely what we were created to do. Under such circumstances, what are we to make of the claim to be objective or disinterested? True, we do not ask ourselves or our students to believe what they read. But the act itself decides matters, and the act is sacred.*

If it is so that learning constitutes a ritual, with argument the chief rite, then does it not follow that the university now is a holy place? For it is there that learning goes forward in a refreshing and engaged classical spirit. We concede too much when we admit that learning under pious auspices is meant to "make better Jews" while learning in a university is intended merely to produce better-informed people. That is so, but it cannot obscure the fact that, as I said, the act itself is sacred. Informedness has its religious effects.

What follows from this is that the university can be subjected to sacrilege, because it is a holy place. By sacrilege I mean the use of something holy for profane purposes, and in the case of the university, the use of the university for purposes extrinsic to its intellectual character and commitment to reason. If people propose in the university to build a "power-base" vis à vis the Jewish community, if they intend to make use of the class-room for the creation of "good Jews," and if they know at the outset of the course the conclusions the students are supposed to reach at the end—about the subject of the course, let alone about themselves "as Jews" or as philo-Semites (!)—those people do sacrilege. And this too is, I believe, consonant with the claim of the tradition of learning in Judaism, that learning is to be for its own sake. We cannot ask of ourselves more than that we competently and informedly interpret what is before us, be sure our students comprehend and understand the texts and their ideas. That work itself is sufficient, just as, in the Temple, the sacrifice sufficed.

It is fairly asked, What about deeds? Is learning without deeds fairly represented here? The answer obviously is that learning without deeds—like deeds without learning—is partial and insufficient. Accordingly, we cannot claim that the university is holy in the way in which the synagogue or the yeshiva is holy. It is not. But so far as what it proposes to accomplish, which is learning for the sake of understanding (and not faith seeking understanding, let alone faith seeking an apology for faith), that partial and impoverished work suffices.

Jewish students and scholars of Judaism nonetheless face a difficult task. It is not one of attaining the requisite measure of objectivity, let alone indifference, hostility or disdain. It is the work of discovering, in what is old and familiar, what is surprising and unexpected. The words we study in the university classroom have been said many times over, so we assume we know what they mean. In fact, unless we realize they are alien words, spoken by people who lived in a foreign world, we cannot begin to comprehend those words at all. It is familiarity which breeds in us not merely boredom, but truly distorted understanding. Because we have heard something many times, may even know it by heart, we assume we understand precisely what it means. We do not ask how to interpret a passage, we take for granted we already know. Yet it is obvious that the words of the sacred texts—even holy books written by nineteenth-century historians and philosophers—speak out of a different age, make use of common words in an uncommon way. We all have been submerged in a stifling apologetic (treated in later papers), and it is this apologetic which has given us the inappropriate confidence of having heard it all.

The real issue facing Jewish students of Jewish religion is not the attainment of objectivity but the realization that the familiar speaks about unfamiliar things and in a foreign language of thought. What is to be besought is a humble sense of the alien and unknown, and to that matter, objectivity is scarcely relevant. For what difference does it make whether we believe or do not believe in, are committed or uncommitted to, what to begin with, lacking proper interpretation, is gibberish? Objectivity is an evasion; the issue is an effect of the historicistic and positivistic modes of scholarly and theological thought in Judaism. For those who find historicism banal and positivism puerile, it is exceedingly difficult to grasp the meaning of objectivity, unless all it means is to eschew propaganda and proselytism, and that is obvious and trivial. The urgency of those who see it as the center of the academic problematic baffles me.

IV

TWO SETTINGS FOR JEWISH STUDIES

I

The Jewish Setting for Jewish Studies

The predominant setting for Jewish studies is the Jewish-sponsored institution. There all members of the faculty and all students are Jewish. What is studied is the Jews and Judaism. Such a setting, by definition, is inbred, for the varying perspectives of non-Jews are excluded, and the achievements of scholarship on other than Jewish subjects neglected.

But the Jewish school is inbred in a second, and deeper sense. Because of the sectarianism of Jewish community life, Jewish institutions are not Jewish alone, but Reform-Jewish, Orthodox-Jewish, Conservative-Jewish, Secular-Jewish and so on. The result is that the faculties are selected mainly or solely from among believers in the school's own sectarian position. Reform Jews tend not to teach at Orthodox and Conservative institutions, and the contrary is for the most part also the case. This inbreeding produces still a third, and most serious sort of parochialism: the faculties tend to emerge from the students so that most members of the Hebrew Union College faculty will have D.H.L.'s or Ph.D.'s from Hebrew Union College, most members of Jewish Theological Seminary's faculty are Seminary graduates, and so on. The professors rarely have experience in teaching in other settings but their own seminary.

The inevitable result of these several sorts of inbreeding is intolerant provincialism: excessive praise for the accomplishments, however trivial, of the ingroup, excessive criticism of the achievements, however ambitious, of outsiders, above all, total indifference to the existence of other institutions of higher Jewish learning, except when, through some accident, they form part of the extended constituency of the home-community. Consequently, Jewish learning until the recent past has consisted of several mutually exclusive and indifferent sets of interlocking 'establishments', each with its own local icons, to be brought forth and gazed upon at ceremonial occasions, each with its proscribed ideas and unread books, each confident of its priority in the scheme of Jewish learning, and each certain of its exclusive possession of truth. The isolation of the several schools is virtually complete.

II

Continuities with the Wissenschaft Des Judentums

What is remarkable is that these several centers for higher Jewish learning, as well as those in Europe and the State of Israel, all trace their origins to the beginnings of the Science of Judaism. The faculties furthermore imagine that they stand within the value-free, non-theological framework of discourse established, they suppose, at the outset of the *Wissenschaft des Judentums* and preserved thereafter. Consequently, they claim to produce "science" and therefore justify the neglect of theology and other value-centered subjects. They see themselves as exempt from the "Jewish question" in its intellectual and social formulations. They do not "believe," for they are engaged in pure learning, philological or textual if possible, at all events objective and historical.

Indeed, the prevalent attitudes of the Jewish scholars employed by Jewish institutions *do* continue those of the founders of the Science of Judaism, who were in a similar social situation and who espoused similar ideas about their scholarly tasks. But those attitudes tend to be insular and pedantic rather than objective and "scientific." The continuities are close, and the parallels exact.

The setting itself obviously has not changed. Just as the Jewish scholar of Judaism in a Jewish institution has little or no contact with the world of the universities, so from the very beginnings— through no fault of their own, but because of anti-Semitism—all the participants in the Science of Judaism were employed by Jewish institutions, either as teachers or as rabbis or in some other sectarian task. It is difficult to locate a single nineteenth-century scholar of Judaism who enjoyed a university appointment. So Geiger wrote to Nöldeke: "To this very day, Jews are all but completely barred from unrestricted scholarly pursuits; much of the work is done either by rabbis who are already overburdened with official duties, or by dilettantes. How could one expect them to produce work of a nature that demands a lifetime of devoted labor?" [1] When one considers the formidable achievements of scholarship in classics or New Testament, one has to recall that scholarship in Judaism was not supported in the same lavish way. While whole platoons of scholars were gainfully employed full-time in New Testament studies, few Jewish scholars in the nineteenth century were able to devote the whole of their working hours to Jewish learning. No wonder their solid achievements are modest in comparison to those in other fields.

But the limitations of the parochial setting went mostly unperceived, except by Moritz Steinschneider. He raised the central issue of Jewish scholarship: Can it be pursued in isolation from other disciplines in the humanities? He answered that it cannot. Steinschneider stressed the importance of knowing about the non-Jewish environment and background. Salo Baron comments: "In contrast to the prevailing 'isolationist' treatment of Jewish history, he tirelessly emphasized that Jewish science and literature can properly be understood and evaluated only in their interrelations with non-Jewish sciences and literatures . . . So conceived, the understanding of the Jewish past required arduous study of the various disciplines and countries. Not sweeping generalizations, but an endless series of monographs was indicated." [2] Steinschneider's advocacy of the establishment of Jewish chairs at faculties at general universities, rather than of separate Jewish theological seminaries, must therefore be seen as part of his scholarly perception, not merely a matter of concern for prestige. He deplored the fact that independent professorships did not exist in the Judaic field in German universities.

Steinschneider held in contempt the isolated pursuit of Jewish studies. In 1875 he referred to the Hochschule fur die Wissenschaft des Judentums as "the new ghetto for Jewish learning." Of still greater consequence, in 1871 Steinschneider declined a position at the Hochschule, stating "that he could not teach there without placing himself in opposition to the statutes of the institution or renouncing his convictions." He declined, in 1876, to accept a position at the Budapest Seminary, saying, as quoted by Alexander Marx: "The subjects which he could teach and his conception of Jewish scholarship would not fit an institution which held itself aloof from the university. He objected to special institutions for the training of rabbis and claimed that they nowadays promoted systematic hypocrisy and scholarly immaturity. What is scientific in Jewish history and literature does not have to fight shy of the universities and should be made available to Christians. He rather favored endowing chairs at philosophic faculties for unsalaried instructors . . . in order to induce the government to establish professorships in this field." [3]

Nor may we ignore the isolation of the Jewish scholars from the Jewish community, a situation which has not much changed in a century and a half. For example, Zunz found himself a stranger to the Jewish community of Berlin: "Thus their ware is without value to me, and mine without value to them."

The modern parallel is two-fold. First, the larger number of Jewish scholars—outside of the social sciences—stands aloof from the Jewish community. The organizations and institutions which constitute that community, to be sure, want little or nothing to do with the scholars, who represent a sort of Jewish authority-figure with whom the leadership cannot cope. The scholar is qualified not by possession of great wealth, nor by an interest in rising through 'hard work' in the community super-structure, nor by charismatic or other spiritual gifts, but only by what he knows. To those who to begin with know little or nothing, the qualification of knowledge and a critical intellect represents no qualification at all. So, as for Zunz, so today, what the scholar has to offer, the community does not want—and vice versa.

Second, the larger number of scholars stands in an ambivalent relationship to the Jews. They make slight effort to address the community, to bring to a wider public the results of scholarly inquiry. They seek no larger constituency for their ideas and values—denying, after all, that they have values and present ideas which are other than "facts." Relationships with the living community are seen as somehow compromising the scholarly objectivity and integrity which they claim for themselves.

III

Theology in Historical Guise

The allegations that scholarship can be carried out free of theological and philosophical questions and that in the history of Jewish learning in the past century and a half Judaica was "purely scientific" contradict the facts of the case. Indeed, from the beginning the founders of the Science of Judaism asserted their freedom from parochial or theological values and also undertook the central theological task facing their own generation. But they did so without the aware and self-conscious consideration of the central methodological issues, so emerged as nothing other than true believers in dogma they claimed as non-dogmatic. Their dogmas, or deeply believed propositions, were not formulated or criticized according to the sophisticated canons of philosophical theology. Rather, the scholars asserted that matters of belief were inconsequential, and then proceeded to posit as fact propositions which were theological statements. Indeed, not only was the theological issue predominant, but the task of scholarship was understood as a fundamentally religious enterprise. Scholarship was made a mode of Jewish expression; it expressed a conviction of commitment and was carried out in a spirit of naive, unself-conscious faith. Its task, moreover, was the definition of Judaism—that is, what theologians were supposed in earlier ages to accomplish.

Nahum N. Glatzer stresses that the founders of Jewish scholarship did not mean "to offer a norm [or direction] for our own judgment," so Zunz.[5] At the same time, the interest in history was not without a contemporary meaning. The historians sought to show that the Jews and Judaism occupied a place within world history. Indeed, the study of history, which supposedly was an objective science, in fact replaced theology and carried out the theological function— badly, to be sure. The "historicistic mode of thinking," Glatzer says, "provided a ready answer to the quest of Wissenschaft des Judentums in its first generations. The issue of doctrine, of the binding character of tradition, of truth, could be safely excluded from investigation. Establishment of historical roots of religious observances helped in the introduction of synagogal and liturgical reforms."

Judaism henceforward could be described by historians in terms of facts rather than defined by theologians in terms of faith. So Glatzer: "Since religious thought lacks an objective foundation and makes for divisiveness, it is better left with the theologians and sermonizers and should not become a subject of scholarship, Zunz felt. It was the tendency of the period to demonstrate points of contact between Israel and the world, even a close relationship between the two, a task undertaken by what may be called 'ideological,' 'theoretical' or 'higher' historicism." [6] So institutions and beliefs were presented relative to their position in history, and the 'higher historicism' would establish Judaism as an integral part of world history. Glatzer concludes, "This almost dogmatic construction came to occupy the status previously held by religion." History was to serve the cause not only of reform and of apologetics, but also of creative and philosophical theology. Glatzer spells this out: "The religious inquiry, an inquiry from within, was replaced by a historicism that attempted to view Jewish history from without. In order to retain the right to exist in the present, Judaism had to be explained in terms of world history, as a community of universal historic significance." [7]

Immanuel Wolf, "On the Concept of a Science of Judaism," written in 1822, states:

> What is this idea that has existed throughout so much of world history and has so successfully influenced the culture of the human race? . . . It is the idea of unlimited unity in the all. It is contained in the one word YHWH which signifies indeed the living unity of all being in eternity, the absolute being outside defined time and space. This concept is revealed to the Jewish people. . . . [8]

He further states, "[The science of Judaism] treats the object of study in and for itself, for its own sake, and not for any special purpose or definite intention. It begins without any preconceived opinion and is not concerned with the final result. . . . Science is self-sufficient, is in itself an essential need of the human spirit. . . ."

The aim of the science of Judaism is to depict "it"—Judaism—as it developed, and then to explain it "philosophically, according to its inner essence and idea." The "philosophy of Judaism" is seen as having as its object "to unfold and reveal in all its truth in accordance with its inner rationality . . . it will point to the connection between external historical events and the inner development of the living idea." The goal was messianic:

> The Jews must once again show their mettle as doughty fellow-workers in the common task of mankind. They must raise themselves and their principle to the level of a science, for this is the attitude of the European world. This attitude must banish the relationship of strangeness in which Jews and Judaism have hitherto stood in relation to the outside world. And if one day a bond is to join the whole of humanity, then it is the bond of science, the bond of pure reason, the bond of truth.

For his part, Geiger divides the history of Judaism into four periods. The fourth, beginning in the middle of the eighteenth century, is the era of liberation. This has been "marked by an effort to loosen the fetters of the previous era by means of the use of reason and historical research . . . What is being attempted is solely to revitalize Judaism and to cause the stream of history to flow forth once again. This is the era of *Critical Study* [italics his], our own modern era." [9] Geiger certainly saw scholarship as the instrument of reform. So he wrote to M. A. Stern (Dec. 8, 1857): "My judgment would be heavily beclouded were I to be deceived in my belief, which is corroborated by additional study every day, that I have discovered the one correct method which will both pave the way for historical insight and truly initiate a continued development based on firm foundations." [10]

Max Wiener lays out the "Ideology of the Founders of Jewish Scientific Research" stressing that the "real motivating force in the Jewish scientific research of the nineteenth century consisted in the adoption of a stand on the question of Jewish survival or in the desire to find satisfaction in such survival." The founders of the Verein fuer judische Kultur und Wissenschaft in 1819 "believed they could not lead an honorable existence either as men or as Jews unless they took stock of the meaning and content of their Jewishness. Scholarship . . . thus became for them the very basis of life. The true expression of Jewish life was to be found in scholarly preoccupation with Judaism." They took as their task the provision for the "modern cultured Jew" of "the potential to carry on as a Jew." They therefore sought to find the "essence of Judaism" so that "they could remain Jews." Finding that "essence" was necessary for the future of the Jews. They therefore sought to define the "idea" of Judaism, and it is revealed by the "national spirit" which is shown "in history as the unity of a multi-varied whole." Gans states, "What this age wants . . . is to arrive at a knowledge of itself. It wants not only to be, but to know itself." Thus we find ourselves in the center of early nineteenth-century philosophy: "Reality must acquire knowledge of itself." To Gans Jewish knowledge was part of general knowledge and should help overcome the Jews' isolation. To Immanuel Wolf, "the Jewish idea" expresses the Volksgeist of the Jews, not religious, but philosophic and scientific truth. And Zunz held, "The moral and social equality of Jews will be the result of the equality of Jewish scientific research." Philosophy would unite the whole and give it meaning, produce a system determined by the "idea" of Judaism. This produced philosophical meaning for purely factual research.

The statements just now adduced in evidence seem to me to demonstrate that the task of the founders of the Science of Judaism was understood by them as nothing other than theology in a secular, scholarly mode. The definition of their purposes, the religious language used in formulating their problems, the central concerns adopted for the scholarly enterprise as these are fundamentally and profoundly theological.

IV

Retrograde Tendencies in Parochial Scholarship

One may further point out that because they worked in isolation from the scholarly issues and achievements of their own day, at least some of the participants in the Science of Judaism claimed as *scientific,* results which were naive and primitive, hardly in accord with the critical achievements of their own day. My examples are drawn from my area of special interest, the historical study of Talmudic and cognate literature.[12] I imagine that in other areas matters are less bleak.

An interest in historical questions is not unique to modern scholars. Those who told historical and biographical stories in Talmudic times and those who later on composed histories based on such stories obviously wanted to reconstruct the past. But until the nineteenth century—and for Talmudic studies until the last third of the twentieth century—it was taken for granted that a story in a holy book about an event accurately portrays exactly what happened. The story itself *has* no "history," but it *is* history. No special interests or viewpoints are revealed in a given historical account. Everything is taken at face value. Since historians and story-tellers stand together within the same system of values, it was unthinkable that anyone would either lie or make up a story for his own partisan purposes. No one ever would wonder, *Cui bono?* To whose interest is it to tell a given story? Obviously, if a learned rabbi told a story, he said it because he knew it to be so not because he wanted to make up evidence to support his own viewpoint. But in modern times—beginning long before the Enlightenment—people learned to take a skeptical position *vis-à-vis* the sacred histories and holy biographies of the earlier generation. They asked about the tendencies of stories, the point the storyteller wished to make, and wondered not about whether a story "really" happened, but rather, about the situation to which a given story actually supplies accurate testimony. They asked how the storyteller knew the facts of the case. Who told him? If he was an eye-witness, on whose side did he stand in a situation of conflict? No reporters were present to take down verbatim what was said and done at the various incidents recorded in the rabbinic traditions. If that is so, then all we have are traditions about such events, given both form and substance on some other, later occasion than that of which they speak. But often we have not traditions but mere legends, fabrications quite unrelated to the events they purport to relate.

Such a skeptical attitude had been well established in New Testament and *Tanakh* studies done by non-Jews by the early nineteenth century. German scholarship in these and related fields furthermore showed the necessity of analyzing the components of stories and asking how each element took shape and where and when the several elements were put together. But with rabbinic materials, aside from some reservations about obvious miracles, one rarely discerns among nineteenth or even most twentieth-century scholars the internal necessity to understand the historical background of texts in a manner other than that narrated in the texts themselves. And when the rabbinic scholars tried to stand outside the presuppositions of the texts, they did so chiefly for exegetical, not historical purposes. Only in recent times have various scholars of rabbinic literature in different ways shown that one must come to terms with the hidden historical agenda and the complex literary situation of rabbinic literature.

But nearly all scholars of the Mishnah produced histories of "the Oral Torah" or "introductions to the Mishnah" which take for granted the historicity of the sayings and stories adduced in rabbinic literature as evidence about the Mishnah's own history.

One cannot, however, attempt to refute histories made up on the basis of Talmudic tales. One can only point out that such histories are seriously deficient, because they are wholly uncritical and gullible, omit all reference to the internal evidence revealed by Mishnah itself, and exclude from discussion the literary evidences available in cognate literature, particularly Tosefta. Nor need one refute the nineteenth- and twentieth-century histories of the Mishnah which, using the Talmudic materials, go on to reinterpret them, to posit new "postulates" about their meaning, to reject one detail of a story in favor of another—in all, to lay claim to a "critical" position toward a literature whose historical usefulness is never in the end called into question or criticized. In such histories we have the pretense of critical scholarship but not its substance. The bulk of the work of nineteenth- and twentieth-century historians of the Mishnah must be regarded as pseudo-critical, critical in rhetoric but wholly traditional in all its presuppositions; and in the main, primitive and puerile. Like the "critical" fundamentalists, who agree that the whale did not really swallow Jonah, but only kept him in his cheek, or like the pseudorthodox who say it was for three hours, not for three days, the "critical" scholars of the modern period have scarcely improved upon the traditional picture. They have merely rearranged some of its elements. Nothing has changed, but much is made of the changes.

Two specific examples of the primitivism of the scholarship of so-called "scientific" scholars will suffice. First, Zecharias Frankel, the founder of the modern study of the Mishnah, is still taken seriously, as shown by the reprinting of his books and their use in contemporary Israeli scholarship to this day. But Frankel operates in a world of private definitions, circular reasoning, and capricious postulates. For him it is unnecessary to prove much, for one may, through *defining* things properly, obviate the need for proof. For Frankel medieval commentaries constitute primary sources for the study of the Mishnah. He furthermore claims that *Seder Toharot* is old because it is the largest order (!); that the ancient Jews were all students of the rabbinic Torah; that the structure of the Mishnah was revealed by divine inspiration; and numerous other marvels. In what way then is he to be regarded as "modern"? The reception of his book supplies the answer. His enemies accused him of treating the Mishnah in a secular spirit and not as a divinely revealed document, the Oral Torah. They said he regarded the Mishnah as the work of men and as a time-bound document. He even explained Mishnaic laws other than through the Babylonian Talmud. For this Frankel was condemned by the traditionalists of his day. That his work today is taken seriously among traditionalists tells us that what is said in the name of tradition changes from one century to the next. But scarcely a line of his *Darkhé HaMishnah* can be taken seriously.

Second, H. Albeck looks upon the Mishnah as the culmination of the process of "oral tradition" beginning in ancient times. He takes for granted that anything reflective of non-Scriptural (= oral) tradition, whether in biblical or apocryphal, pseudepigraphic, or Septuagintal literature, is *The Oral Tradition* of Pharisaic-Rabbinic Judaism. While Albeck is critical of earlier students of the history of the Oral Torah, he does not depart from their frame of reference. Indeed, Albeck takes pretty much the position of Sherira Gaon, founder of Talmudic history, altering details but not the main points. What is striking is that for Albeck the scholarly agenda formulated by Sherira remain uncriticized and unchanged: "When was the Mishnah written?" He extensively reviews and criticizes the ideas of earlier scholars, as if they had supplied him with viable agenda. So we find ourselves once again in the midst of debates on the work of the Men of the Great Assembly, although we have not the slightest shred of evidence about what they had actually done, let alone a document produced by them or in their days. While Y. N. Epstein demonstrated, for example, that the tractate Eduyyot was produced by the disciples of Aqiba at Usha—they are explicitly named throughout—Albeck takes seriously what the traditions from Talmudic times allege, that Eduyyot was produced at Yavneh: "It was ordered according to the names of the sages and the work was done at Yavneh." But he never proves this is so. One may easily show that Eduyyot is *different* from other tractates, but that difference does not mean it is *earlier* than the others. Whatever a Talmudic tradition alleges about a tractate is taken as fact. Albeck seldom looks in a thorough and critical way for internal evidence. Again and again one finds circular reasoning. For example, Albeck holds that Rabbi arranged the material he had received according to a single principle: content, and he did not change anything he had received. How do we know this? Because Rabbi ordered the material only according to the content of the laws and any material not collected according to this principle was formed into units before Rabbi received them. We know that they were formed into units in Rabbi's sources because Rabbi ordered his material only according to the content of the laws. Likewise, Rabbi did not change any of the material he received because the sources are not changed. We know the sources are not changed because Rabbi did not change any of the sources. And so forth. Albeck further disputes the view of Epstein that the Mishnah yielded numerous variations in texts. He says once the Mishnah was edited, it was never again changed. I am not clear on how Albeck understands the work of the early Amoraim, for they seem not only to have changed the Mishnah, but to have stated explicitly that they changed the Mishnah.

Though separated by a century, Frankel and Albeck exhibit the same credulousness and lack of critical acumen. Considering the achievements of scholarship in the intervening hundred years, one may be astonished at how little Albeck's perception of the critical task and definition of the problems has been affected. But Frankel, too, exhibits little mastery of the critical conceptions of his own day.

V

The Novelty of the University for Jewish Learning

Shortly before the First World War, sixty leading German theologians and philologists, including Noeldecke and Wellhausen, petitioned the Ministry of Education to establish a chair for Judische Wissenschaft.[13] The War prevented realizing the "removal of an old injustice," but in Weimar times, a series of lectures by Jewish scholars was arranged at the Institutum Judaica of Berlin University in the years 1925–1926, and these were published in 1927. It is difficult to imagine that such a lecture series was seen as a major step forward. Today Jewish studies are widely and in a few places seriously pursued in universities. Without firm statistics in hand, I may allege that at least as large a number of scholars of Judaica is employed in universities as in Jewish institutions. The first important change in the development, over the past decade, of the university as a major center for Jewish learning is the exponential increase in resources available for the field. The aggregate investment on the part of universities of their own uncommitted funds, in addition to moneys received from outside, chiefly Jewish, sources for that purpose, is apt to have doubled the number of positions open to full-time professionally qualified Jewish scholars.

That fact has led to a second development, not entirely welcomed by the Jewish institutions. The parochial schools now have to compete both in financial and in less material terms with the universities. Until now they could maintain to their students, many of whom study or had studied in secular universities, that the way things are done in the Jewish class-room is the only way Jewish studies can be done. Now students may compare the way in which they are taught in university class-rooms—including those devoted to Jewish learning —with the way in which they are taught in Seminaries. Since the Jewish schools tend to preserve the worst part of the legacy of the East Euopean *heder* and *yeshivah,* the comparison is apt not to be favorable.

Still a third salubrious development is the end of the control of a relatively few individuals over the development of the careers of younger scholars. Since power of placement now is vastly diffused, it is possible for people with quite new approaches to old problems as well as with new definitions for worthwhile inquiries to make their way. A measure of the resentment on the part of the older and established faculties in the parochial schools is the statement to this writer, "Just because a university board of trustees has declared a person to be a Jewish scholar, that does not make him a Jewish scholar at all." The assumption was that the consenus of the sages and that alone would have to suffice. But in point of fact innovative careers now are possible which ten or fifteen years ago would not have led to a living in the profession of Jewish learning.

Fourth, in consequence the hold of old approaches and old ideas no longer is taken for granted, unless it can be shown that those approaches and ideas constitute the best ways of seeing things and solving problems. Not only new methods, derived from well-developed disciplines formerly without impact upon Jewish learning, but also new areas of interest are accepted as legitimate. They have to be, for their practitioners enjoy university professorships and are able to support themselves by their scholarly efforts and teaching.

VI

Toward the Future

Obviously, I follow Steinschneider in wondering about the future of what he called "ghetto-learning" and what I regard as an essentially parochial setting for Jewish scholarship. One wonders what scholarly achievements will be possible among men whose appointments depend upon criteria irrelevant to scholarship, what educational environment will be created in dogmatic surroundings where —as among future-rabbis—the question of relevance and the search for instant wisdom are predominant considerations. Until now whatever talent was available had perforce to accept the parochial setting of Jewish learning. But that is no longer the case. Will the Jewish schools find themselves able to compete for talent, even among their own graduates, with the opening up of hitherto undreamt-of opportunities for true intellectual freedom and a genuinely heterogeneous scholarly climate? If the study of cognate languages and the larger setting of Jewish history and culture is central to the task, and it is generally acknowledged by all but obscurantists that it is, how then will the parochial schools overcome the intrinsic parochialism of their curriculum and faculty? If the disciplinary aspect of learning is shown to be fructifying, and it is, then how will the parochial schools cope with their heritage of generalism and unprofessional acquaintance with an excessively wide, but shallow, range of knowledge? If Steinschneider is right that no aspect of Jewish learning can be pursued in isolation from the corresponding setting in the larger culture, then what future is there for parochial departments of Jewish studies whose curricula ignore the existence of the universities of which they are a part? These seem to me difficult questions.

These are not my problems. But the university-situation is so utterly novel in the history of Jewish learning, its openness, heterogeneity, variety, and educational challenges so unprecedented, that a whole new set of problems is to be faced. The questions of the place of values and commitments, the issues and methods appropriate to the new setting, the definition of a viable curriculum or set of curricula useful to the university's needs, the relationship of forms of Jewish scholarship pursued in various settings to one another, the formulation of new scholarly agenda and areas of specialization—all of these questions are as yet unanswered, and, given the exceptionally brief career of Jewish learning in universities as an autonomous setting for study, unanswerable. My contention is that the university as a primary locus for the pursuit of Jewish scholarship—not merely as the place of employment for two or three eminent individuals—is unique, unprecedented, and apt to produce still unanticipated results. But I cannot claim to predict the nature, still less, the value, of those results.

FOOTNOTES

1. Cited in Max Weiner, ed., *Abraham Geiger and Liberal Judaism* (Philadelphia), 1962, p. 136, letter of July 8, 1872.
2. *History and Jewish Historians* (Philadelphia, 1964), p. 278.
3. *Essays in Jewish Biography* (Philadelphia, 1948), pp. 144-5.
4. Nahum Glatzer, ed., *Leopold and Adelheid Zunz. An Account in Letters. 1815-1885* (London, 1958), p. xxv.
5. "The Beginnings of Modern Jewish Studies," Alexander Altmann, ed., *Studies in Nineteenth-Century Jewish Intellectual History* (Cambridge, 1964), pp. 27-45. This is an exceptionally valuable synthesis.
6. *Ibid.,* p. 35.
7. *Ibid.,* p. 44.
8. *Publications of the Leo Baeck Institute of Jews from Germany. Year Book II, 1957* (London, 1957), pp. 194ff.
9. Quoted in Weiner, p. 156.
10. Quoted in Weiner, p. 121.
11. *YIVO Bleter* 29, 1947.
12. This analysis is drawn from Jacob Neusner, ed., *The Modern Study of the Mishnah* (Leiden, 1972: E. J. Brill). Further materials on the modern study of Talmudic history are assembled in Jacob Neusner, ed., *The Formation of the Babylonian Talmud* (Leiden, 1970: E. J. Brill).
13. E. I. J. Rosenthal, *Studia Semitica.* Vol. I, *Jewish Themes* (Cambridge, 1971), p. 338.

COMMENT

Perhaps the critique offered in this paper is too sharp. Colleagues who teach in Jewish theological schools insist that their courses are "value-free" and "objective," and that there is no difference between their modes and purposes of instruction and those of scholars in universities. If that is so, then one wonders whether the seminary professors take seriously the tasks entrusted to them. For their students are, in the main, going to be rabbis and teachers and to carry forward the work of advocating Judaism. They have every right to expect that rabbinical education will prepare them for rabbinical careers. They must acquire understanding and appreciation for Jewish religion as well as a philosophy of Jewish life—a theology— shaped out of the resources of Judaism and relevant to the spiritual situation of the Jewish people. Accordingly, seminary professors who see themselves as "value-free" repudiate the purposes of the colleges and seminaries in which they labor. These colleges and seminaries lay claim upon the support of the Jewish community precisely because they are not "value-free," but because they stand for and advocate Judaism.

But, as is stressed here, the claim to be "value-free" and objective is proved not merely inappropriate but also spurious. For when we examine the scholarly conceptions nurtured by Jewish scholars teaching Jewish students in Jewish seminaries, we discover remarkable continuities between the conceptions about history and literature advanced by the tradition about itself, on the one side, and the conceptions about history and literature put forward as "objective" and "scholarly" by those parochial scholars. The methods and disciplines of contemporary historical and literary-critical studies simply are not understood, the urgency of the critical agendum shaped over the past two hundred years is not perceived, and sources are evaluated and constructed into historical accounts without undergoing the sort of critical study which is old and routine in universities. As I said, the consequent picture of "exactly what happened" turns out to be remarkably similar to the picture of the history of tradition advanced by the tradition in its own behalf. All that changes is the claim put forward in behalf of that picture. It is not the claim of faith, of belief in the veracity of ancient fables, but now is the claim of history, of "merely" knowing "the facts." This is the grievous price paid by Jewish scholars of Judaism for their intellectual in-breeding and provinciality.

It is, as is claimed in this paper, "theology in the guise of history," and it is historicist theology masquerading as positivist scholarship. The negative consequences are two. First, as is argued here, a heavy price is paid in historical knowledge. What the sources can tell us and do prove is ignored. Proper interpretation is impossible. Second, the still heavier cost is in the loss of the religious dimension, the foreclosure of the possibility of piety and faith. For if all we have are facts, then what need, what room is there for faith at all? Jews do not "believe" because the propositions of faith are mere facts, and they are not supposed to experience the attitude of faith, trust, hope, and joy in God, for that experience depends, to begin with, upon openness to things which are not facts at all. The negative effects of a positivism and a historicism preserved beyond their time lay in the deadening of the spiritual capacities of the religious intellectuals—scholars and rabbis themselves.

True, at the outset, historicism solved a pressing problem, the dilemma of intellectuals emerging from one age of the Jewish spirit to another, determined to hold on to what had gone by, but through new means. But their students, and their students' students, lived in still another world. For them the problem was not, and is not, the intellectual reform of an enduring and vital intellectual tradition. It was and is the recovery of the capacity to participate in the past and dead tradition, which means to begin with, to comprehend precisely the vividness of the issues of the tradition itself. If all we ask of the tradition is whether it really happened, we miss the point of the tradition itself, which in its classical formulations never really claims authority on the grounds of reporting and describing things which really happened, but of believing things which are true because God said them. Scholarship found itself impoverished because of its hostility to piety and religiosity and so prevented scholars from understanding and appropriately interpreting the materials subjected to scholarly inquiry.

At the same time, the results of scholarship so represent Jewish tradition and Jewish religion to the Jewish people as to deprive the people of an important part of their birthright: the right to believe despite the world, against the facts of the world. Consider the existential tasks of the Jewish people, small and unimportant, yet hated out of all proportion to its weakness and insignificance. Does that people not require faith against that hostile world and confidence despite it? Historicism offered the opposite: the pretention of power and normative cognitive status claimed in behalf of the people and its faith by positivism. In solving the problem of one generation, the founders of the Wissenschaft achieved rightful immortality. But in gaining for their solution prestige out of all proportion to their concrete achievements, the founders of the Wissenschaft laid a heavy lien against the spiritual future of the Jews.

That is why the unpretention, the true objectivity, and the wholly value-free position espoused by Steinschneider are so admirable. He took seriously the work of universities, evidently far more seriously than did those who controlled the universities. He understood the work of scholarship as separate from the work of theology, an amazing intellectual achievement in the light of his circumstance.

Yet if Steinschneider had found his place in a university, I wonder whether he would have found the new setting without its problems. At the end of this paper the author claimed to be free of discussing those problems, because the setting is without precedent and experience is brief. Yet should he not have seen—and stated—those failures which already had become clear, and by now, in just a few years, are already notorious? I refer specifically to the superficiality of the curriculum, the resort to fads and the neglect of the hard work of learning required for meaningful insight, characteristic of the American liberal arts college and university in general, and of the study of Judaism within the humanities curriculum in particular. Have we so much of which to be proud, who see a given student for one course in one semester and leave him with unfounded confidence in his wisdom—and in ours? I think not. In the struggle with the old, established way, the writer lacked the requisite honesty to point up flaws in the new path. Some of these are endemic, as I said, but that does not excuse them. Others are not necessary at all, yet are commonplace. Chief among them are intellectual pretentiousness, disdain for hard work, that same search for instant wisdom, phrased in different ("academic") terms to be sure, characteristic of the old setting. It should be said with appropriate emphasis: the university indeed is a new and unprecedented setting for Jewish learning, but we do not know, and have no reason to believe, that it is a better setting. *Only solid achievements in education and scholarship will show that it is a better setting. Presently, all we have is an opportunity.*

Part Three

THE ACADEMIC STUDY
OF JUDAISM

THE ACADEMIC STUDY OF JUDAISM

Introduction

The two papers in this unit focus upon one aspect of the academic study of Judaism as a religion. It is the study of Judaism from the perspective of the history of religions. The first paper treats the issue within a theoretical framework, distinguishing between the results of history, on the one side, and of history of religion, on the other. The second covers much more ground, defining the academic study of Judaism, suggesting topics important primarily in theological, not secular academic settings, differentiating between attitudes appropriate in the one setting as distinguished from the other, and finally explaining, in fairly general terms, some of the issues brought to the study of Judaism and its history by historians of religions. Much more is to be said on this topic than is suggested here. But this programmatic paper may be helpful in providing a way of organizing inquiry into the subject.

The two papers in this section were originally written for academic conferences, the first at the University of Iowa on methodology and world religions, the second at Princeton University on religions in the university curriculum. Both therefore address scholars in the fields of religion and history and take for granted a rather considerable corpus of values, experiences and academic problems held in common. When the second paper was read by people in Jewish theological settings, so far as there was a response, it was to the argument against "Jewish history," as I said, and that was a surprise. For that point was passed over as routine and obvious at the Princeton conference, at which discussion centered on quite other matters. That fact underlines the difference, insufficiently appreciated within Jewish theological schools, between the givens of discourse in universities and what is taken for granted in seminaries.

71

V

THE STUDY OF RELIGION AS THE STUDY OF
TRADITION IN JUDAISM

To begin, let me choose among available definitions of "religion." I find congenial the one offered by Van A. Harvey (*The Historian and the Believer* [N.Y., 1966], p. 258-9), "A religion . . . may be regarded as a perspective, a standpoint, in which certain dominant images are used by its adherents to orient themselves to the present and the future . . . a way of looking at experience as a whole . . . a way of interpreting certain elemental features of human existence." I find this definition congenial because it lays stress, as Harvey's context requires, on the cultural aspect of religion, making room for the collective imagination as well as for the discrete mind, for society as well as for the individual, and for the accumulation of events we call history, as well as for the present moment. For Judaism, the cultural, the societal, and the historical constitute primary and formative categories. No definition of religion which fails to stress these aspects of religious phenomena is going to suffice.

Yet the intellectual, individual, and immediate, or contemporary, side to the religious life cannot be left out. When we consider the central religious experiences of Judaism, we find the definition of the faith in terms of tradition, but tradition understood as paradigmatic experience perceived to be vivid and very present. That is to say, experience of the perfect and eternal, lived in the here and now, joined to myth which describes and reshapes ordinary life in the model of that experience of eternity or of the sacred, together constitute tradition. The Passover *Haggadah,* which, after all, is simply an exegetical exercise in the Deuteronomic conception of Israel's life, makes that fact explicit. *"We* were slaves of Pharaoh in Egypt." The stress is on those present, not on some long-dead ancestors. "If God had not brought our fathers forth from Egypt, then surely we, and our children, would be enslaved. . . ." The generations are three: our fathers, we, and our children—immediate past, present, and immediate future, in accord with the perceptions of living people, for whom great-grandparents and great-grandchildren are scarcely a reality. This then is underlined in the parable of the four sons, which begins with the wicked one, who asks, "What is all this drudgery of yours for?" And the narrative proceeds, "Mark the words and the tone, 'This drudgery of yours,' as if he were not one of us." "Answer him in the spirit of his question, "All this I do because of what God did for me—for me, not for you." And there follows: "This is the promise which stood by our forefathers and stands by us, for neither once, nor twice, nor three times was destruction planned for us. In every generation God delivers us from their hands." And, at the end, "For ever after, in every generation, everyone must think of himself as having gone forth from Egypt, for we read in the Torah, 'In that day thou shalt teach thy son, saying, All this is because of what God did for me when I went forth from Egypt.' It was not only our forefathers that the Holy One . . . redeemed. Us too, the living, he redeemed together with them. . . ."

These passages could be duplicated, in one form or another, throughout the religious experience of Judaism, and the counterpart of their spirit is to be discerned in the secular writings of contemporary Jews as well. They show that a religious tradition, claimed to be among the more historical traditions, also exemplifies the vivid contemporaneity of tradition, the capacity of tradition not solely to preserve dead experience, but to shape and endow with meaning ordinary everyday life in the present. We err in regarding Judaism as primarily cultural, societal, and historical—traditional—in its focus. So far as Judaism is a living faith, it is personal, mythical or intellectual (in a broad sense), and acutely contemporary.

Yet what is important to the historian of religion in the Judaic religious life is the stress on tradition, and what is distinctive in the study of Judaism is what it teaches us about the study of traditions as an aspect or mode of the study of religions. Let me now define what I do not mean by tradition. I do not mean by tradition, "Something which is handed on intact from one generation to the next." I do mean, "something handed on from the past which is made contemporary and transmitted because of its intense contemporaneity." Tradition involves both the giver and the taker, backward in time and forward as well. It imposes a dynamic relationship, a creative tension, between the remote past, with its authority based on a myth of revelation, as we shall see below, and the remote future, with its power vested in the capacity to continue to vivify, or to abandon and thus kill, the received legacy. Let me give two examples of what I mean by tradition.

The first derives from a just completed research of mine on Eliezer ben Hyrcanus, a first-century rabbi. What I found, as I dissected traditions, or authoritative sayings, attributed to Eliezer in accord with the later generations' references to what he was alleged to have said, is that the several strata of tradition were strikingly interrelated. If an early follower of Eliezer alleged that he gave a ruling, a later tradent—one who participates in the formation and transmission of tradition—would likely do one of two things. Either he would refine the substance of that ruling. Or he would hand on in Eliezer's name a ruling either spun out of the principle established in the original saying or closely related to it. I found out that it would be highly unlikely that to Eliezer would be attributed a saying with no roots whatever in the primary and original corpus of teachings assigned to him by the circle of his contemporaries and disciples. That seemed to me an unexpected result, an example of how disciplined and principled was the formative process of tradition. So by "tradition" in this sense we may understand, the developing out of the teachings of an early authority the logical principles, and, from them, the necessary consequences for later times. Tradition in this sense is living, yet, as I said, accurate and careful, mindful of what has gone before. It is not capricious, not subjective, not ahistorical, not indifferent to the facts of the past.

My second example is drawn from a story about how a major

authority served a meal to his underlings. One version of the story justifies this action as follows:

> The Holy One . . . causes the winds to blow and clouds to ascend and rain to descend . . . and prepares a table before every single person, and as regards ourselves, should not Rabban Gamaliel [patriarch of his day] . . . stand and serve drinks to us [b. Qid. 32b].

The other version reads:

> The Holy One . . . gives to everyone according to his needs . . . and not to fit men and righteous only, but even to the wicked, worshippers of idols. Concerning Rabban Gamaliel, how much the more so is it fitting that he stand and serve drinks to sages and sons of Torah [Mekhilta Amalek, Horovitz-Rabin pp. 195-6].

What is striking is that the first version stresses that God serves man, so the authority serves *his* servants in the model of God. The second, by contrast, says that since God serves the fit and the unfit, so all the more should Gamaliel serve masters of Torah and sages—who alone are *fit*. This is an example of how a tradition not only is carried on, but also may be made to serve the theological and polemical needs of a later generation. In this case, a fairly standard story about divine beneficence is turned into an apologetic for the authority of the rabbis, even over their own leader. The story is made to state that serving the rabbis is an act in imitation of God. In the first instance, we are told that just as God serves the world, so the patriarch, Gamaliel, should serve the world. In the second, a drastic revision has God serve both the righteous and the wicked, so Gamaliel, the patriarch, at the very least should serve the sages—a very different message. I tend to think the first story is the earlier one, and to find the differences in the second evidences of revision, at a later point, in behalf of an important rabbinical polemic.

As we noted, tradition involves both the giver and the taker. What the literary instance just given shows is how the tradition proves vital, serviceable for polemic and thus for the discussion of contemporary issues, long after its original theme and form are established. The "giver" here is the storyteller who has handed on a little pericope about how the patriarch, in serving his guests, imitates God, who serves nature. The "taker"—the one who revised the story—then has turned the story into something relevant to his particular and distinctive concerns. Tradition as process of handing on and passing forward thus is dynamic and not static. Its interest is not in what was originally said alone, but in how what was said in the past endows with meaning, imposes sense upon, the issues of the new age. Tradition is killed when handed on unchanged. It is vivified when it goes forward, while not intact, fundamentally unimpaired.

These two examples of a living tradition tell us a great deal about the study of Judaism as the study of traditions and their history.

First, we learn that the study of Judaism involves the study of literary materials, by contrast to the study of living liturgy, with its gestures and symbols, processionals and music, which enjoys vividness without encapsulation in words. The study of Judaism requires a wider focus than is commonplace for the study of theology, with its stress on abstract theological ideas, and with its imperfect capacity to come to grips with those ideas which do not yield abstraction, with the substance of myth or of law, for example.

Second, we learn that the study of Judaism involves reflection, in particular, on the sayings and stories of men who were important legal authorities (for the issue in the story of Gamaliel is whether it is proper to do such-and-so). So the focus of the tradition is not on indiscriminate materials which have been handed down, but on a very particular type of information, sayings and stories about what people are supposed to do.

Third, we learn that the study of Judaism involves the study of the *history* of traditions, for it is clear that in the transformation of materials—their interpretation in later times, their revision in terms of the interests of later generations—we are going to locate the essential traits of the tradition as process. That is to say, if you want to know about Judaism, you had better ask not about its condition at a given point in its history (especially not about its condition in contemporary times), but rather about its dynamics, its continuing processes, its 'progress' through time. To learn what is distinctive about Judaism one will want to ask about those permanent traits and trends which, from age to age, turn out to speak to and for the accumulated tradition, on the one side, and also to and for the living generation, on the other.

The examples I offered of the vital tradition teach two facts. First, as I stressed, the tradition is not capricious, does not assign, without grounds or reasons, a saying to an ancient authority, merely because a living person would find it useful for that ancient authority to have stated such a saying. Second, the tradition does make room, through the processes of retelling and reinterpreting the tradition, for the most current concerns. The 'rabbinization' of the story about Gamaliel, the intrusion of "rabbis" and "sages" where the original account knew nothing except about nature and "all mankind," shows us how a story might be reworked for the theological interests of its tellers.

Now one question is deeply inappropriate for the study of such traditions, and that is, did this story really take place? The intense concern to locate the actual words of a given authority, to be able to make a determination of whether or not something really happened, commits outrage upon the materials of a tradition. For those materials to begin with do not allege concerning themselves the sort of historical interest, let alone historical accuracy, implicit in such a question. The contrary is the case. When we tell of what a great authority said or did, we speak of eternities and of the sacred. We mean to say, This is how holy things *are,* not how, once and for a single, finite moment, they were. The point and purpose of tradition are not to pass on historical facts, but both to create and to interpret contemporary reality, to intervene in history. The tradents' interest in the past is solely because of its paradigmatic value, not for its authority over the present in some lesser, banal and factual sense. The past is not dead, is not past, specifically because it is paradigmatic.

But if the past is paradigmatic, then the past is perceived not as "historical" but as very present. Then what of the claim that Judaism (or Christianity, or Islam) is a "historical religion"? What indeed can we mean by a "historical religion"? I think what has been meant is this: Judaism is not a religion of myth, a religion which tells stories about things which did not actually happen, but which recounts events which really did take place. Why should that claim be important? I think it was important to historicistic theology, which proposes to replace matters of "faith" with statements of "historical fact," so to solve the crisis of conviction confronting nineteenth- and twentieth-century Jews. By claiming that Judaism (among other allegedly historical religions) did not deal in faith but in facts, the challenge of positivism would be met—by complete surrender. But I argue that that theological statement about Judaism as a "historical religion" is simply false on the face of it, leading to a profound misinterpretation of the meaning of "being Jewish." And the historicistic theory of authority misinterprets the theory of authority behind tradition in Judaism, as we shall observe shortly.

So far as we ask about the traits and definition of a religious tradition, therefore, we want to know about the process and perspective, the standpoint and dominant images, used by adherents to orient themselves to the present and future. That inquiry is the opposite of the historical one. True, to gain an accurate picture of the way in which a tradition works, of its dynamism, we have to ask many historical questions. But these questions are not properly framed solely in terms of whether the tradition is "true," with truth measured by historical verifiability. Rather we want to know whether and how tradition changes, and the way these changes reveal what is taking place in the imagination of the people who took up the tradition and turned it into the center of their being. Tradition serves as the mode of orientation toward the present and future, as the way of interpreting existence, not because it tells us where we have been, but because it explains who we are, what we are, where we are, and whither we should go.

Let me return to the living 'tradition' of the Passover *Haggadah,* which I introduced at the outset. The stress is that "we were slaves and now are free." God saved and saves *us,* not them, the dead, alone. The son who asks, "What is this to you?" is wicked. But what makes the ritual of the bitter herbs and the unleavened bread, the myth of the exodus from Egypt, into vivid and intensely meaningful experiences is their perceived correspondence to the contemporary experience of ordinary folk throughout the history of the Jewish people: "Not once nor twice nor three times was destruction planned for us." The experience of a small people, scattered throughout the world, facing in every generation the fact of alienation and differentiation from the rest of society—that experience, whether or not accompanied by oppression and destruction, as in our own day, is made intensely meaningful because the people are able to see themselves as reliving what has long passed. They therefore are able to seek for themselves the redemption which, they hope and believe, is just as permanent, just as formative and paradigmatic, as is the experience of alienation and oppression. People are able to see themselves as having gone forth from Egypt because they know in their everyday life what it means to be "slaves to Pharaoh in Egypt." The universality of that experience, the omnipresence of the yearning for the passage "from slavery to freedom, from anguish to joy, from mourning to gladness, from darkness into light" is shown by the capacity of these same images to embody the experience of so many other peoples.

The historian of religion differs from the historian, therefore, in his study of traditions. He asks a quite separate set of questions. His inquiries, in my view, are more appropriate to the nature of his evidence. What he wants to know is not solely whether the Israelites really went forth from Egypt, but what the belief that the Israelites really went forth from Egypt teaches us about the history, culture, and society of the people for whom that fact of life serves as a paradigm and explanation for contemporary reality. The historian of religion treats historical events as utterly contemporary in their meaning, whatever period in the history of the tradition concerns him. He understands that every tradition is a historical fact. Someone told a story. Whether or not the story is so, the telling of the story is itself a tremendous fact, and deserves most serious interpretation. What we know from the telling of the story is a whole set of facts about the mind and imagination of the teller, about the society to whom he told the story, about the cultural realities to which the story was deemed pertinent and which were reflected (one may take for granted) in the details of the story. It is sufficient, therefore, to know the history of a hero—that is, the ways in which his life was narrated and interpreted in times long after his death—

without asking whether said hero did and taught what he was supposed to have done.

Let me here cite an extreme example of the gullibility and child-
ishness of the historical hermeneutic. There is a saying in the Talmud, told about Hillel, "One day, walking beside a stream, he saw a
skull, and he said, 'Because you drowned others, you were drowned.
And those that drowned you will be drowned.' " I need not dwell
on the philosophy of this saying. What have the historians done with
it? A debate, the participants of which will, mercifully, remain un-
named, raged for some twenty years about the identity of the person
whose skull Hillel saw, the day on which Hillel saw the skull, and
the events which led up to the person's being drowned. Along the
same lines, we have a story that Hillel came up from Babylonia to
the land of Israel. This saying is in the context of a comparison of
Hillel to Ezra, that is, of Hillel as law-giver. The point is fairly clear.
The story tells us that the people who told it saw the founder of their
movement as equivalent to Ezra, who revived the life of the community of Jerusalem just as "Hillel"—that is, the later followers of
Hillel—proposed to give a new Torah and so refound the life of the
community. But a historian figured out that Hillel came up from
Babylonia on the 15th of March in the year 30 B.C. and proposed,
in all seriousness, that the anniversary of that "event" be celebrated
by contemporary Jewry. That is one way in which historians try to
serve the mythopoeic function of the ancient storytellers. The sage's
cloak does not fit.

It is the perspective of the history of religions which liberates the
sources from the straight-jacket of historical studies, narrowly construed, and opens the way to the study and interpretation of traditions in a way congruent to their own purpose and point. For no one
in the religious tradition proposes to preserve what happened solely
because knowing what happened matters, without attention to its
larger and wider meanings. The conviction that raised facts about
the past from antiquarianism to value-forming and society-shaping
knowledge is peculiarly Western, and, in the main, Protestant. Yet
that very concern for the past—for "just what happened"—resulted
less in a sympathetic understanding of what had happened, than in

an effort either to judge the past or to make use of its facts in the vindication and verification of the contemporary world-view. As A. Leo Oppenheim states (*Ancient Mesopotamia* [Chicago, 1964], p. 30), "The humanities have never been successful in treating alien civilizations with that tender care and deep respect that such an undertaking demands. Their conceptual tools are geared to integration on their own terms and to assimilation along Western standards." Anyone who doubts the justice of Oppenheim's critique of Assyriology pursued by humanists had best read the studies of Judaism carried out by Protestant, Catholic, or Jewish theologians, nearly all of them exercises in theological apologetics in the cloak of historical science and in the guise of scholarship.

The reason, I think, is that historical studies tend to take for granted their original, uncriticized ideological foundations. These are based upon the simple conviction that one must distinguish "whether or not something actually happened, whether it happened in the way it is told or in some other way . . ." (August Schlegel, quoted by Harvey, *op. cit.,* p. 4). When historians come to non-Western civilizations, they come with a considerable agendum. Assyriology began "at the moment when Western man was eager to step out of that magic circle, the field of energy that protects, preserves, and confines every civilization . . . Western man became . . . willing and able to appreciate and to evaluate with objectivity his own civilization, to correlate other civilizations, and to strive for an understanding of some over-all design and plan . . . " That is the point at which not only Assyriology, but the whole range and spectrum of historical sciences, took shape.

This curious concatenation of events in the history of Western consciousness—the concern for what "really" happened, on the one side, and the search for self-consciousness through the inquiry into what happened in other than the known Western and Protestant setting, on the other—stands behind the study of traditions for narrowly historical purposes which goes on today as it has in the past. It accounts, too, for the intense interest in that vexed question, the personality, character, and teaching of the "historical Jesus." For the theologian lacking faith in the Christ of faith, the search, for purely scientific and completely disinterested, objective historical motives, for the historical Jesus seemed a happy way out of the dilemma of preserving an essentially religious heritage in the absence of religious conviction. If it could be shown that the Jesus of history really said such-and-so, then the authority of that saying would be established, taken for granted. Why there should be much difference between a saying believed for eighteen centuries to have been said by Jesus and one pronounced as genuine by the authority of historical science was never clearly spelled out. Rather, it was taken for granted that the authority of the saying rested with the authority of the one who said it. If one could show Jesus really said it, then that sufficed. The circle of faith, if broken, could be restored. The authority of Jesus could be taken for granted, if history could show he exerted authority. It was merely a different way of arguing about the effects of that authority—through the transmission of tradition or through the determination of the historian. In other words, the historian who would determine what Jesus really had said, in the assumption that the fact of his having said it made all the difference, is not easily to be distinguished from the theologian. Both take for granted what someone outside the circle of faith does not, namely, that the question is important, the answer somehow determinative, normative, or authoritative.

I do not claim that the task of finding out, as best we can, just what happened is unimportant or secondary. The interpretive task of the historian of religions wholly depends upon the prior accomplishment of the scientific task of the historian. Before we know two things, we cannot interpret anything: first, who told a story, to whom, and under what circumstances? Second, whether and in what degree does the story correspond to an actual event? These are narrowly historical questions, and before we know the answers, the heuristic task is premature. For the beginning of interpretation is to know *who* and *what* it is that we are to interpret, whether we have a fantasy, or a fantastic view of reality, or a mundane statement of an everyday event. Every tradition constitutes a historical datum, a fact, and it is for the historian to supply the historian of religions with the description, the facticity, of that fact: its setting, its veracity,

above all, to what and to whom it testifies. I am in entire agreement
with my colleague, Horst R. Moehring, who states, "Any historian,
whether 'just' a historian or a historian of religion, must first of all
understand the material with which he is working. The interpretation of an event will have to be determined differently, if critical
research shows that it never happened in the way in which it is pre-
supposed in the interpretation." My criticism of historicism is not to
be understood as a rejection of the achievements of historians, but as
a complete affirmation of their method and results, together with the
warning not to exceed the just limits of those results. It is the historian who makes theological statements, like the biologist who makes
philosophical ones, that is here viewed as ludicrous. Both claim to
an authority not conferred by the method or results of sound, positivistic inquiry. For both, facts are asked to transcend themselves,
information is asked to surpass its intellectual quotient. Let history
be history, let theology be theology, and let historians of religion re-
flect upon both—and more.

Having many times referred to the "authorities" of the rabbinic
tradition and just now criticized the view that historical events are
"authoritative," I find it is time to face squarely the issue, What is
the nature of the authority of tradition? If, as I claim, merely because something happened, it is not therefore authoritative, then on
what basis is "tradition," viewed as suggested here, regarded as
"normative"?

We begin with the theologico-mythic answer of Rabbinic Judaism.
The "tradition" is normative because it was revealed to Moses at
Sinai; the Torah is God's will for Israel, and the contents of the
Torah comprehend both the written Scripture everyone knows and
the Oral Torah *handed on as tradition* at the same time: "Moses
received the Torah from Sinai and handed it on to Joshua. . . ."
The two key words meaning tradition, QBL, received, and MSR,
handed on, occur in that weighty sentence. In post-biblical Hebrew,
there are two ways of saying tradition, *qabbalah* and *massoret*. The
nature of the authority of tradition then is clear: it derives from
God's word to Moses, called *our rabbi*. Central to the concept of
authoritative tradition, specifically of Torah, therefore, is the view

of Moses as the authority, the *rabbi,* who stands behind the Pentateuch and the Oral Torah of the later rabbis. To ask, at what point
and how does *tradition* become authoritative, therefore, we must ask,
When is Pentateuch claimed to be Mosaic? Where does the concept of Moses as the archetypical and prototypical rabbi emerge?
Above all, what is the alternative authority, over against that of the
tradition of Moses?

E. J. Bickerman recently pointed out[1] that it is with Philo that the
Mosaic authorship of the Torah becomes axiomatic. While Moses
as author of, and authority behind, Scriptures or sacred revelations
occurs earlier, I think it is clear from Bickerman's observation that
the authority of Moses becomes important in the Judaism of the last
century or so before 70 A.D., and that that importance, specifically,
is to Hellenistic Judaism. In the Rabbinic Judaism, taking shape
after 70, the figure of Moses similarly is exceedingly important. Yet
in the rabbinic traditions about the Pharisees before 70, Moses occurs
in not a single saying, apart from the opening sentence of Avot cited
above. Further, the earliest versions of the chain of Pharisaic tradition beginning with that sentence know nothing of Moses, Joshua,
elders, and prophets; these are added only in the last chain, which is
unlikely to derive from the period before 200 A.D. It is at that
same time that the Mishnah itself was promulgated, under the claim
that it contains the Oral Torah of Moses, enjoying the same normative and authoritative status as the written Torah, the Pentateuch.
The claim that the tradition was handed on orally, through memori-
zation, begins after, and not before 70, and becomes well attested
only after 140.

My colleague Horst R. Moehring points out the meaning of these
facts, that Mosaic authorship of the Pentateuch is strikingly important, first, to Alexandrian Judaism, and, second, to the rabbis after
70, with particular prominence coming after 140. The answer lies
in what the two groups—Alexandrian Jews, post-70 rabbis—have in
common. It is temporal or spatial distance from the Temple of Jerusalem. While the Temple stood, for Jews living in the land of Israel
it was the fount of authority. The reason, however, was its place
not merely in the administration of their affairs, but in the shaping

of the sacred canopy under which they lived out their days, by the stars of which they navigated the course of life, so to speak. The centrality of the Temple in the mythic life of the people may be shown in many ways. One, just now important in my work, is the view that all forms of purity and impurity are referred ultimately to the Temple, which indicates, as Mary Douglas argues, that that is the point on which the lines of authority, social and cosmic, converge.[2]

It is with the collapse of the Temple as the organizing force of society and ordinary affairs—either because of distance, with the Alexandrians, or because of the unavailability of the cult, after 70, and of the obviously permanent end of the cult, after 140, that we find growing importance attached to the figure of Moses. Moses the mystagogue or the rabbi, for the pre-70 Alexandrians or the post-70 rabbis, respectively, now stands behind tradition, whose authority depends upon its origin with Moses—and with God. Formerly, the Temple cult provided the center of the organization of reality. Now God does—through Moses' Torah. The tradition of things gone by which still endure takes its place.

I therefore offer an entirely historical explanation for the authority of tradition in rabbinic Judaism, simply by pointing to the time at which the change in the basis of the existence of society and of the interpretation of reality took place. Yet it should not be understood as an essentially historical explanation. For what is important is not the time of the destruction of the Temple. Philo and perhaps some of his predecessors show the physical existence of the Temple is not at issue. What I think is important is a change affecting many groups in Greco-Roman antiquity, where Temples were closing not solely by reason of destruction, where new modes of relating to the divinity were taking shape. As Jonathan Z. Smith observes, it is at that same time that magicians became important; the substance of their magical actions commonly involved an act of sacrifice.

What is the nature of the authority of tradition in Judaism? The answer is first given in the mythico-theological language of Rabbinic Judaism itself, then accounted for the point at which that language became significant. Tradition is authoritative because it comes from

Moses, therefore from God, an idea especially important in the century after the destruction of the Temple. The authority of the "authorities" of the Rabbinic tradition rests upon their holding, embodying, and handing on the Torah of Moses, a Torah conceived in God's image. The rabbi therefore stands as the paragon of Moses "our rabbi" who imitated God, his rabbi. The authority of the rabbi is based upon the myth that the rabbi exemplifies God's image, is holy like God. The Temple and the cult exhibit the earthly model of the heavens; the rabbi, priest and mystagogue, carries forward the ancient mode of authority.

What of "Torah" or tradition, within the proposed interpretation? It seems to me clear that "Torah" takes the place of the earthly Temple in the functioning of the Jews' social and political life, on the one hand, and of the cosmic Temple in the articulation of their imaginative world and expression of the sacred on the other. The foundation of the authority of tradition must then be compared to that of the authority of Temple, a comparison which we cannot fully undertake within the narrow framework of our present problem.

Finally, let us ask about the role of history of religions in the study of tradition. History of religions, with its sympathetic interest in the wide range of religious traditions, with its capacity to recognize the historian-of-religions' own situation, and to take account, in the interpretive task, of the stance of the interpreter himself, has the capacity to turn the study of traditions into something of significance for the study of the larger issues of religion. The reason, as is already clear, is that the historian of religions has the capacity to take seriously and in its own terms the importance of tradition, without asking the reductionist question of whether tradition really is right about the people alleged to have participated in its formation or to have served as the object of its rule or teaching. The accumulation of story, law, wisdom, and theology preserved in the tradition is a rich resource for the understanding and interpretation of the cultural history of a religion, but only when allowed to stand as a fact in itself. For the tradition—its shape, its development, its modulations through time—testifies with unfailing accuracy, as I said, to the mind and imagination of the people who gave and continue to give it that shape, who nurture that development, and who effect those modulations.

This, I think, is to be taken as fact. But for the historian of religion, the discovery of the people to whose perception of the sacred the tradition *does* testify as a matter of fact does not constitute an end in itself. Once we have located the people who stand behind traditions, unlike historians we have begun, not completed, our work. The historians then tend to reduce the facts, purported to be contained in traditions, to the interests and prejudices of the people who hand on, therefore who stand behind the distortion of, those facts. But the historian of religions is not interested solely or even primarily in what really happened in the period of which the tradition speaks, but rather, in what we learn about the people *to* whom the tradition speaks.

Yet among historians of religion, one notices a curiously limited range of interests. Many scholars of early Christianity bore us by their intense, repetitive interest solely in whether Jesus really said something. Some of them pronounce the bulk of Jewish tradition pertaining to the period as "worthless" because it does not help them recover what Jesus really said or did not say. But historians of religion, I think, exhibit a parallel, if less paralyzing, narrowness of interest, in one sort of religious data, those deriving from studies of symbols. Their definition of religion in some measure may be derived from an examination of what they regard as the worthwhile result of their inquiry. Let me take as an example the late Erwin Goodenough, whom I revere. Goodenough took as his task the interpretation of the symbols found in the archaeological remains of ancient Judaism, and his primary interest—beyond the brilliant scholarship required for his work—lay in the interpretation of the universal appeal or meaning of those symbols. This he found in their salvific symbolism. Virtually every symbol found in ancient Jewish art was shown ultimately to bear salvific valence, to serve as a means of expressing the devotee's yearning for salvation. To establish the correctness of this interpretation, Goodenough therefore had to distinguish between the specific meanings associated with a given symbol in its own setting—that is, the verbal explanation found in the literature referring to such a symbol—and the larger, universal meaning, *not* given verbal explanation but latent in the imagination of anyone exposed to such a symbol, to be located in the parallel appearances of said symbol in other cultures. Consequently, Goodenough took slight interest in the rabbinic literary data. These, by definition, were adjudged irrelevant to the task of the interpretation of Jewish symbols. He drastically limited the range of his interpretative possibilities, on the one hand, and equally radically limited the range of data with the interpretation of which he would concern himself, on the other. This is what I mean by a certain narrowness of interest on the part of historians of religion. It derives, obviously in the case of Goodenough, from the sense that part of the task of history of religions is to compare religious data, and from the recognition that the task of comparison must be considerably facilitated by the location of those elements of a given religious tradition which may be freed of their specificities and concrete location in an incomparable setting, a concrete culture.

A religious tradition, however, is not to be limited to its nonverbal aspects, on the one side, or to those myths of such obviously universal significance as to make possible the task of comparison, on the other. It must be taken whole and complete, determinative on its own of what is important and of what is "religious." So far as we take seriously Harvey's stress on religion as a way of interpreting certain elemental features of human existence, we have to understand as *religious* whatever in a given tradition functions as part of such an interpretative enterprise. Accordingly, even the interest in history itself has to be subsumed—even reduced—to its significance in the interpretation of the mind and self-understanding of a given religious community or society, our own. The historical hermeneutic, which assigns importance to something in relationship to whether the historian can persuade himself something has really happened, testifies, after all, to the positivistic hermeneutic of a given setting. Similarly, history of religions needs to take seriously the quintessential, revelatory nature of law in Judaism, or of purity rites in Zoroastrianism, Hinduism, and Judaism, as much as of the structure of the Buddhist

Temple, the character of the Islamic creed, or the Christology of the Roman Catholic Church.

All religious data, and not merely those data pertinent to myth and ritual, are to be subjected to the historian-of-religions' mode of interpretation. It is history of religions which has repeatedly claimed the urgency of preserving the concern for what is religious about religion, without engaging in the reduction of religion to an aspect of history and culture, of psychology and sociology, or of metaphysics and philosophy. Then history of religions has likewise to take seriously the religious meaning of the study of tradition and the results of that study. This is in two aspects. First, place is to be found in the history of religions for the results of those who, like myself, think much of consequence is to be learned from the history of the growth and continuity of a given religious tradition. And, second, place is to be found among data thought worthy of interpretation by history of religions for the fact that, in Judaism at least, the *study* of the tradition itself is an act of profound religious consequence.

FOOTNOTES

1. E. J. Bickerman, "Faux littéraires dans l'antiquité classique, en marge d'un livre récent," *Rivista di Filologia e di Istruzione Classica* Vol. 101, 3rd series, 1973, 1, pp. 22-41, in particular, pp. 34-5.
2. Jacob Neusner, *The Idea of Purity in Ancient Judaism* (Leiden, 1973), with a critique by Mary Douglas, and Mary Douglas, *Purity and Danger* (London, 1966).

COMMENT

The central thesis of this paper, that Judaism is an ahistorical religion with its myths about Abraham, Sinai, and redemption, is fairly challenged by a two-fold criticism, which I owe to Professor Amos Funkenstein, University of California at Los Angeles. First, people honestly believed these things did happen and did distinguish between fable and history. Second, people did preserve a sense of the past-ness of the past, a sense of the distinction between themselves and what had gone before, so as to deprive the past of its authority, therefore its mystic quality. My stress on the contemporaneity of tradition is not in the tradition itself.

This is, as I said, a fair criticism. For it underlines the subterranean historicism present in the claim that past events do possess authority, do compel the reaching of conclusions about the present. That is the center of the historicistic claim. It may therefore be true that all that is achieved here is a restatement of that claim in other language. Yet the evaluation of the criticism derives, I think, not from the facts of whether Jewish theologians before modern times distinguished between what actually happened (within the limits of historical science of their day) and figurative stories or fables (in Philo's sense). It is, rather, a problem in the interpretation of the way people are moved to action, the abiding traits of the spiritual situation of humankind. It is a judgment about ourselves, therefore, which must be made. How do we perceive the human condition, in particular, our own imaginative and mythopoeic capacities?

When we contemplate the ineluctable power of certain stories about the Jewish people—stories about redemption from Egyptian bondage, about Sinai, about the messiah, about the holy land and holy people—we have to ask the source of that power. Is it simply because something happened long ago that we look forward to its happening once again? Or is it because we perceive an urgency, a fittingness, to what happened then and can and must take place again? I think the power of Israelite and Jewish myth to reshape the imagination of many peoples far outside of the Jewish situation testifies to the universal humanity, the eternal contemporaneity, of stories about slaves who are freed, pilgrim people who seek and find a land, sinning, suffering people who atone for sin and are forgiven and restored to their land. If people see themselves in such terms, it is because of traits intrinsic to recurring existential circumstances, slavery, suffering, alienation and the sense of exile. Historical events—whether they truly happened as the fables say they did, or whether they appear to us to have happened because they conform to our imagination of the world—never possess authority merely because they took place. Their authority, their capacity to evoke in us assent and conviction, depends upon their fittingness to our situation, not our submission to their claim.

The old myths, phrased in the conventions of historical tales to be sure, so shape the contemporary Jewish imagination that even "secular Jews" respond to them. No better evidence of that fact is to be adduced than the popular response to the destruction of European Jewry (called "The Holocaust") and the creation of the State of Israel (called "the beginning of our redemption"). Why is it that the one should be seen so securely tied to the other? Part of the reason, to be sure, lies solely in the sequence of events and in the natural, and I think correct, view that the one made the other necessary. But part of the reason lies in the incapacity of people to cope with the one without the other, the necessity of finding some meaning in the endless suffering of European Jewry. Yet why should people have taken for granted there must be any meaning at all, surely any meaning referring beyond this world? Why, further, should people have used the language of religion and especially of salvation when viewing this-worldly events? Why should they have interpreted reality, as they have, in categories corresponding so exactly to the language and categories of the salvific myths and yearnings of Judaism? It is that self-evident correspondence which to me is persuasive testimony to the contemporaneity of the Judaic myth. For precisely the Jews most sure that this world is all and there is no other are those who dedicate themselves most wholly to the work of, and for, the State of Israel as a sacred—the only sacred—task. The deeds themselves, it is fairly argued, are secular and this-worldly, conforming to the practical requirements of our century. But what of the explanation of those deeds, the interpretation of reality which leads people to do them? Try as I might, I am unable to comprehend how that interpretation derives wholly from this world and from the here and now.

That is not to suggest that Professor Funkenstein's criticism is without merit. It is only to propose an angle of interpretation of the problem itself. If the whole truth is that people did and do distinguish between myth and history, then what is the force of that distinction? If they did and do preserve a sense of the past-ness of the past, of history as a wholly secular set of facts, then why does the past shape their imagination and interpretation of the present, as I think it evidently does? We have yet to locate among the Jews a wholly and totally secular perspective, except among those Jews who have entirely left the Jewish situation and no longer respond to the things Jews think are important. Whether they have then entered some other framework of belief and interpretation, in place of the one they have abandoned, is something I do not claim to know.

VI

MODES OF JEWISH STUDIES IN THE UNIVERSITY

Learning constitutes a central religious category in Judaism. From the earliest days of Pharisaism almost to the present time, "study of Torah" predominated, in various forms, in shaping the values of the Jews. The present-day academies in which "Torah" is studied claim descent from schools first founded in Palestine well before the third century B.C. and in Babylonia in the second century A.D. The books written in those schools and the conventions and canons of inquiry originally laid down there continue to occupy students in traditional schools. Among the intellectual traditions which took shape in the Middle East in late antiquity, the Jewish one thrives much in the old way, as well as in new forms, and represents one of the longest unbroken chains of learning among men, along with Confucianism and the study of philosophy.

The advent of the study of Judaism in American universities must be seen from this perspective. Judaism is no parvenu in the world of the academy. The scholar whose main task is the study of Judaism may be a relative newcomer in the American university, for until the late 1950s only a few faculties provided for appointments in the subject of post-biblical Jewish learning. But there is nothing at all novel about scholarly study of, or within, Judaism. If a scholar has received sufficient training in the classical tradition, its sources and methods, then he has become a new representative of a very old discipline. I stress this point, not because antiquity by itself confers any great prestige, but rather because today some Jews celebrate their "acceptance" by the universities of America, as if they had done little or nothing to deserve it. Given both their reverence for learning and veritable awe of the learned man, and also the persistence of these religious traits in cultural and secular forms, they bring to the university a rich appreciation of its central tasks, and their tradition makes its contribution as well. But the university as we know it is only the most recent, and at present not by any means the most important, setting for the enterprise of the Jewish intellect.

My purpose here is not to argue the thesis that Jewish studies belong within the university curriculum, but rather, first, to analyze briefly what these studies comprehend, second, to distinguish between modes of Jewish learning in universities and in Jewish schools, and finally to adumbrate the place I believe appropriate for Jewish studies within the study of the history of religions. A second, equally important place, in Near Eastern studies, is not under discussion here.

Definition: What Is Included in University Studies

We must first carefully define the various modes of Jewish learning so that we may be able to distinguish those germane to universities and those most useful in parochial, Jewish schools. It is clear that the wide range of Jewish studies exhibits a mixture of presuppositions, methods, and topics of interest. Not all of these would contribute to university studies of religion. Furthermore, it is obvious that, when Jews study themselves and their own traditions, they naturally rely upon unarticulated assumptions and exhibit implicit attitudes which require specification. After examining the several definitions for Jewish learning, we shall then be in a position to separate the aspects of Judaic studies appropriate for universities from those best cultivated in Jewish seminaries.

What do we mean by Jewish studies? To answer this question, one must define "study of Torah," *Wissenschaft des Judenthums,* "Hebraica," "Hebrew studies," "Judaica," "Jewish learning," and other terms used to denote the subject under discussion. Of these terms, the broadest is "Jewish learning," which includes the systematic study of the beliefs, actions, and literary and cultural products of all persons who have been called, or have called themselves, "Jews" (of which more below). Within "Jewish learning" one may discern several fairly distinct categories. First is "study of Torah," the traditional, religiously motivated activity, developed over the centuries and focused upon study of the Talmud, commentaries, legal codes, rabbinic interpretation of the Hebrew Bible, and similar sacred sciences pursued in classical Jewish academies and seminaries. Second is "Hebraica" or "Hebrew studies," the study of the Hebrew language, biblical, cognate, and, more recently, modern literature, and related subjects, which was undertaken in American universities and Protestant divinity schools from the very beginning, and now continues in departments of Near Eastern languages and literatures, linguistics, or comparative literature. Third is "Judaica," the systematic study of Judaism, its history and theology, law and practices, and of the Jews as a group, generally carried on in departments of religion or in the social sciences. Of these modes of Jewish learning, the third is the one that will be discussed here. The divisions within "Jewish studies" are rarely demarcated by such clear-cut boundaries as those I have suggested. In general, university programs in "Jewish learning" are divided between Near Eastern and religious studies.[1]

Adequate definitions for the terms "Jew," "Jewish," "Judaism" and "Judaic" are required as well. The study of Judaism includes its philosophy and theology, religious literature, art, music, law, and history; a "Judaic" study focuses upon some aspect of Judaism as a religion. The study of the Jews concerns the culture, sociology, politics, languages, art, literature, and other artifacts of the distinct historical group of that name. That group is composed of people who were born of a Jewish mother, or converted to Judaism. I offer the definition of the Jew given by Jewish law. One may broaden it slightly by adding that a Jew is one who thinks he is, or is thought by others to be, Jewish, with the qualification that such belief is not based upon mistaken facts. Whether or not one may isolate qualities which are distinctively "Jewish" is not at issue here.[2]

In this definition one must stress the importance of change. Qualities or features which Jews borrowed from other peoples in one setting frequently became rooted in Judaism or Jewry, so that later on, or elsewhere, they came to be seen as peculiarly Judaic or Jewish. The Jewish calendar, that "unique" construction of Judaism, derives mostly from the Canaanites. It may be argued that the festivals were "monotheized" or "Judaized," but in fact different verbal explanations have been imposed on the same festivals celebrating the same natural phenomena of the same Palestinian agricultural year. In the early days of Reform Judaism, it was thought that, if one uncovered the "origin" of a practice or belief, he might then decide whether it was "essential" or peripheral. Nowadays there is less interest in "origins." The exposure of the "genetic fallacy" may have been part of the reason for this shift: it was quickly recognized that determination of the "origin" does not exhaust the meaning of a belief or practice. Yet there was another source as well. For it has been progressively more difficult, with the advance of scholarship, to discover *any* deeply "Jewish" or "Israelite" practice which was not in some degree the creation of some other culture or civilization. The Jews, over long centuries, have assumed as their own what was produced originally by others, and their infinite adaptability has been made possible by short memories and tenacious insistence on the mythic-Jewish origins of purely gentile or pagan customs. Whatever was or was not Jewish, a great many things have *become* so.

So far I have not alluded to peculiar Jewish disciplines or methods of study, although these exist, some people suppose, in Talmudic dialectic. That dialectic, however, is formed of Roman principles of legal codification and Greek principles of rhetoric. Probably one could find numerous parallels among contemporary Syriac, late-Babylonian, and Hellenistic traditions, if these were sufficiently well known to us, just as the Jewish academies have their parallels. Although a discipline may be peculiar to a tradition of learning and still be derivative, I doubt that Jewish learning can be associated over a long period of time with any particular discipline, in the sense that sociology has its methods, or physics its procedures. Obviously Jewish learning can lay no persuasive claim to exclusive possession of subtlety or cleverness, devotion to the intellectual life, dedication to "matters of the spirit," or any of the other traits—pejorative or complimentary—claimed for it by its religious and secular enemies or apologists.

"Jewish learning," broadly construed, is most nearly analogous, in university terms, to an area study, in which various disciplines, drawn from the humanities, such as philology, art history, musicology, or literary criticism, and from the social sciences, such as political science, economics, sociology, or the like, are brought to bear upon a certain region, or nation, or segment of society. "Jewish learning" does not necessarily fit into a special department, though "Judaica" appropriately belongs in a department of religious studies, "Hebrew studies" or Hebraica, in a department of Near Eastern languages, and "Jewish studies" pursued from a historical or sociological perspective in a department of history or of sociology and anthropology. Just as many methods may be profitably applied to the study of a geographical region, so also many methods may be used to elucidate aspects of the study of the Jews as a group or of Judaism as a religion. Specialists in various areas of Jewish learning may be located in different departments. In addition, *centers* of Jewish learning, in which specialists from several disciplines may be brought together to work on the Jewish and Judaic materials, ought to be created, where feasible, in some universities. Such "institutes of Jewish studies" would be analogous to the Russian Institute at Columbia and the Middle East Institute at Harvard. On the other hand, a *department* of Jewish or Judaic studies seems to me a misnomer, for departments normally take shape around particular disciplines or approaches to data. Even though departmental and disciplinary lines are breaking down, it is still important to structure Jewish studies in universities according to appropriate existing principles of academic organization.

So far as it is necessary in the beginning to select certain modes of Jewish learning for university purposes, I think two are primary: concentration in Hebrew language and literature for Near Eastern or comparative literature departments, and in the history of Judaism for departments of religious studies. I see no role whatever for the Judaica specialist in the study of contemporary philosophy, though of course studies in the history of philosophy will require his contribution. The social scientist normally makes use of all kinds of data, deriving them from many different cultures, traditions, and social groups, without specializing in any of them. I should suppose, therefore, that the various social sciences, especially anthropology, sociology, and psychology, would find the inclusion of a "specialist in the Jews" egregious and wasteful.

Whether history belongs to the social sciences or the humanities, I see a limited place for the Jewish historian *as such* in a history department. In the past, to be sure, general histories of the Jews have been written, and one might thereby be led to suppose that "the Jews," as a single entity (or "people") existing in various times and places, have had a single history, in the same way as England or America, or China has had a history. It seems to me that the normal inquiry of historians proceeds on the assumption—whether upon geographical, or political, or sociological grounds—that what one is dealing with is a single entity which has had a history. To suppose that "the Jews" constitute such an entity or "people" requires, first of all, assent to a theological or ideological judgment. Once that step is taken, however, the morphology of one's further studies has been established. Whether or not it is congruent with that of historical studies is an open question.

A specialist in Jewish history presumably must be trained not merely in historical *method,* but also in the data pertaining to his field, data which in the Jewish case extend over more countries, cultures, and centuries than most scholars are capable of mastering. The specialist in Jewish history who works in late antiquity has to reckon with Jews who spoke several languages and lived in several different political systems, who wrote many kinds of books, preserved afterward among many different and conflicting groups, each of which claimed to be "the Jews" or "Israel" from that time forward. When the Jewish historian proceeds to medieval studies, he must once again face the variety and breadth of Jewish data, and so too in the modern period. Whether or not a single historian can specialize in "the Balkans" or "the Middle East" and achieve the mastery of the many languages, literatures, and histories demanded of him, I think it unlikely that the same could be done in a thoroughly professional manner with the Jews. Both unarticulated ideological or theological and technical or methodological problems stand in the way of Jewish history.

If, on the other hand, a scholar working, for example, mainly in medieval European history specializes in Jewish materials, as another may stress Germany, or Italy, or Poland, he may make a very significant contribution. For he becomes acquainted at the same time with the broader cultural and social environment which shaped the lives of all people, including the Jews, in medieval Europe; he deepens his understanding of the various political and economic systems governing all groups in a given territory, including the Jews; and he learns about the literature, religion, and other aspects of the civilization of those among whom Jews lived over a period of several centuries. He is, in other words, dealing with a specialty within a broader field of historical research, just as others do. He is not expected to do more than anyone else can reasonably ask of himself. He can become an expert, and, reaching the frontiers of knowledge at a few specific points, he may cross over into unexplored territory.

I do not see how the thirty or forty centuries generally included under the rubric of "Jewish history" can be adequately studied by any one person, and I do not think professional scholarship can cope with so broad a temporal range of study, even within a relatively narrow frame of reference. The need to know the whole of a single period will prevent the historian from knowing the rest of the history of the Jews. In larger faculties, where several men may concentrate upon a single period, such as medieval or modern Europe, there should be a specialist in Jewish material, just as there is in French, Italian, or Russian. But, in general, Jewish history seems to me a less manageable field than the history of Judaism (of which more below). The contrary expectation supposes that the study of Jewish history may safely exclude careful attention to the affairs of the societies among which Jews were living. The presupposition is that these affairs had little or nothing to do with Jewish religion, culture, sociology, literature, and the like. From the Canaanites to the Americans, massive testimony to the contrary has accrued, with variation, but without exception. It is, moreover, a theological judgment to include in Jewish history the study of "normative Jews" and their culture and to exclude the history of others, such as various sorts of Christians, Karaites, and Sabbateans, who from their origins on have claimed to be "the Jews" or "Israel." Whether or not such a judgment can be made, it certainly ought to be made—and put into effect —by *historians*. So there is, or should be, no such field of specialization as Jewish history and, hence, no place in a department of history for a specialist in Jewish history. Places obviously should be found for a medievalist, or a modernist in European or even American studies, and certainly a specialist in ancient history, who works mainly, though not exclusively, on Jewish sources. All those who do specialize in the nonspecialty known as Jewish history in fact end up, as is entirely proper and necessary, concentrating on a particular time period and geographical region, and frequently on only one aspect of Jewish history of that circumscribed time and place.[3]

Modes of Jewish Studies Outside the University: Study of Torah

What is the relationship between university-based Jewish studies discussed above and studies in a Jewish school? The place of Jewish learning in universities is necessarily conditioned by the universe of discourse existing within the university. The university attempts to bring into relationship with one another many kinds of area studies and many sorts of disciplines, in both the humanities and the social sciences. In the context of this heteronomous discourse within the university, various bodies of knowledge contribute to the elucidation of questions of common interest. Under these circumstances Jewish studies are required to concentrate on those elements that are of interest to other disciplines or areas. But the classical tradition of Jewish learning contains many elements that are of no interest at all to outsiders. Pursued for their own sake, that is to say, as an autonomous body of tradition and knowledge dependent upon no other scholarly tradition and no other body of questions or perspectives for validation or relevance, Jewish studies have quite another type of existence. Seeing matters from this standpoint, we may come to a clearer understanding of the relationship between a given area of study and those who actually *live* in the area which is under study.

Within the community of the faithful, Jewish studies from Pharisaic times onward have focused upon the study of the traditions regarded as having been revealed at Mt. Sinai to Moses (according to Pharisaic belief) in both oral and written form. The written revelation is contained in the Pentateuch and, beyond that, in the prophetic books and the writings supposed also to have been written under divine inspiration. The oral tradition was finally written down in the form of the Palestinian and Babylonian Talmuds, various collections of Scriptural exegeses known as *Midrashim,* and cognate literature. Other literature produced by Jews in the long period from Ezra to Mohammed, circa 440 B.C. to A.D. 640, was not preserved by the Pharisaic and rabbinical schools and was not therefore included within the scope of the term "Torah." From the Islamic conquest of the Middle East and the subsequent fructification of all fields of human thought, "Torah" expanded, even in rabbinical circles, to embrace the disciplines of philosophy and metaphysics. From the tenth century to the fifteenth, a vigorous philosophical tradition took shape under the impact of Moslem rationalism. Still a third mode of pre-modern Jewish studies existed in the form of Kabbalah, the Jewish mystical tradition, which conceived of "Torah" under a wholly new guise, as an arcane doctrine of metaphysical mythology. A fourth form was the legal and ethical tradition. This was pursued, first, through commentary upon the Babylonian Talmud, second, through legal research resulting in the issuance of a *responsum* (a letter in reply to a specific legal question), or in the provision of a court decision, and, third, through the construction of great codes of Jewish law, bringing up to date and organizing by specific principles the discrete corpora of laws then being developed in particular countries and by various authorities. A fifth form, which was liturgical and in a measure belletristic, resulted in the composition of a great body of poetry, both religious and secular, in the Hebrew language. A sixth was Bible study and commentary. Of the modes of Jewish learning in pre-modern times, biblical-Talmudic studies were by far the most common; the others existed in small and relatively isolated, uninfluential circles, except at specific times and for local reasons.

The birth of *Wissenschaft des Judenthums* among the nineteenth-century German Jews who had received both a classical Jewish and a university education added to the range of Jewish studies several modern sciences. These were, specifically, history, philology, textual criticism of the classical texts, and biblical studies in the modern mode.[4] New, also, and of greater importance, were the attitudes of complete freedom of interpretation as well as, in Glatzer's words, of "freedom from the possible application of the results of scholarship to the conduct of life." A further change, Glatzer points out, was from the exegetical to the abstract mode of discourse. No longer were books called "contributions toward" or "comments on," but instead major comprehensive projects were undertaken. Most recently, sociology and contemporary history have begun to take root in a particularly Jewish academic environment. Furthermore, books formerly ignored by Jews but preserved by Christians, such as the biblical apocrypha and the New Testament, Josephus, Philo, and the like, have reentered the framework of Jewish learning in modern times.

What unites classical and modern sciences of Judaism are the convictions, first, that such an entity as a "Jewish people" exists, which permits one to study as a *unity* the literature, history, and other cultural artifacts of people who lived in widely separated places and epochs; second, that sufficient unity pervades the culture so that one may meaningfully write a history of Jewish (as opposed merely to modern Hebrew) literature, or a history of the Jews, or similar compositions; and, third, that scholarship concerning "the Jewish people," its culture and religion and history, even its languages, is intrinsically important and interesting. Most significant of all, Jewish studies carried on in an autonomous framework presuppose not only their own intrinsic interest and importance but also their worth in molding the values of the living generation, whether these be religious or secular (*Wissenschaft des Judenthums* was not a university discipline—though it aspired to academic status—but the creation of the early Reformers of Judaism who, despite disclaimers, intended through it to point the way toward the future development of the faith.) Jewish studies in Jewish institutions, therefore, are pursued not simply because they may illuminate some aspect of the humanities or social sciences but, especially and immediately, because they will help the Jewish student to form his beliefs and values by reference to the tradition of which he is a part, or, more descriptively, which shaped his forefathers in various ways.

In my view, any cultural or religious tradition has the right to be taken seriously in its *own* terms, and especially by those to whom it addresses itself. It is not enough to study the traditions and lore of the Jews as aspects of humanity, or because they may provide significant insight into the human condition, as I once argued. The rhetoric may be appealing to some, but the results are disastrous to scholarship. All specificities, all boundaries, all possibility of commitment are quite properly destroyed when the particularities of Jewish learning are subsumed under, and then blotted out by, the perspectives of the humanities or social sciences. It is one thing to study Yiddish, Judaeo-Arabic, Judaeo-Persian, or Hebrew at various points in history because they represent interesting data for the linguist, a valid and important perspective. But it is quite another to study the various languages Jews have regarded as Jewish in order to come to a deeper understanding of their values or of the way their languages generate and interpret visions of reality, or even in order to learn to express oneself through them. The linguist may learn to make use of one of the many languages he studies; the philologist may penetrate into the deeper meaning of a word; but only the committed student and his equally devoted teacher want to *use* that language and find a deeper means of self-expression through that use. Yiddish or Hebrew may well be studied by linguists or Orientalists, respectively, but the value of studying them is quite different, more personal and, I think, more profound, when believing Jews in an autonomous and self-contained setting learn them. Jewish studies represent a heteronomous body of learning; but they also constitute an autonomous tradition, with its own claims and value statements. To ignore the latter is to render impossible the success of the former.

I argue, therefore, that certain kinds of Jewish studies belong within the university curriculum, others only within Jewish institutions of higher learning (such as seminaries and institutes for advanced study), and some in both. Rather than specify particular branches of Jewish studies appropriate for each setting, this essay will develop the particular criteria in terms of which judgments should be made. To take one example: the Talmud deserves to be studied—forever, I hope—in the classical, dialectical manner. It was composed with just such study in mind, and when deprived of the richness of commentary, scholastic disquisition, and the search for new insights in the perfectly traditional, old-fashioned modes, it loses its integrity. That is to say, study of the Talmud must be "study of Torah." But at the same time the Talmud is a historical document. Thus it may be viewed as a resource for philological and cultural studies, as evidence for the state of religion, economic life, sociology, and politics in ancient times, and as a repository of values which in various ways have continued to guide the life of the Jews. For social scientific purposes, the Talmud (as much as the Church Fathers) provides data of great interest for inquiry in the tradition of Max Weber and Ernst Troeltsch, to name only two sociologists of religion. I see no connection between classical Talmud study and the university curriculum, but many relationships between Talmudic literature and various university studies in both the humanities and social sciences. To generalize, potentially each branch of Jewish learning has a contribution to make to university studies, and the criterion for incorporation into the university curriculum will be the possibility of applying university methods of study to the particular subject matters(s).

I think it unfortunate that the success of Jewish studies within the university rests, as it has for a century, upon that of Jewish studies outside it. The mastery of the necessary languages and classical disciplines required for advanced scholarship in Jewish materials cannot be acquired in a few years or in a few courses. Jewish learning demands too deep an education for advanced work to be undertaken upon a foundation presently existing in university curricula alone. Today, therefore, Jewish studies, both in the history of Judaism and in the languages, literature, and history and sociology of the Jews, depend upon extra-university resources. At the present time it may well be advantageous for the scholar of many Jewish subjects to be a Jew in origin and upbringing. The insufficiency of university facilities, and not the intrinsic character of the subject, is the cause. I think that the university must fully carry out its responsibilities, so that a person entering with no background in, or even contact with, the subject may within the normal period of years emerge as a suitably qualified scholar. Thus the university will preserve its own autonomy and achieve that self-sufficiency which in the end will protect and maintain its character. No subject taught in a university must ultimately depend upon foundations laid outside of it. Of course, university-based scholars of Judaica must make maximum use of the substantial achievements of modern scholarship, which has produced the translations, concordances, critical texts, and scientific commentaries needed to provide somewhat easier access to documents, mastery of which would otherwise require a lifetime of study.

On the other hand, one can hardly consign extra-university Jewish learning to the sterility or boredom of the old issues, forms, and procedures. The same problems which led to the development of contemporary humanities and social scientific scholarship within the university are just as troublesome outside of it. Indeed, the philological, historical, social scientific, and other methods hammered out in the past century provide as useful a tool for analysis of a text in a seminary classroom as in a university. One may, of course, continue to ask the old questions and carry out the old procedures. Proof of this possibility derives from the actuality of Jewish learning in more than a few Jewish institutions of higher learning. But the old questions seem less troubling, and the old answers of diminishing persuasiveness. If we find a key to treasures of insight, it should open many doors. The newer modes of learning need, therefore, to reshape the older ones.

The difference between modes of learning in a university and in other centers of study should be made explicit. Scholars in universities do not differ from their counterparts in Jewish-sponsored schools of higher learning in commitment, concern, or protagonism. But the focus of commitment and concern is radically different. The university scholar seeks understanding of structures, the parochial scholar (and I do not use the word pejoratively) seeks participation in them. In a university, commitment is to the scholarly method or result; in a parochial institution, to the content of what is studied. In a university, concern is for humanity or society first, to a particular segment or example of it second; in the parochial institution, concern is for the group first, mankind afterward. Protagonism in the parochial institution is taken for granted. In the university, one advocates scholarly alternatives; but the act of advocacy of a religion as such will impede the comprehension of a religion other than one's own, and I suspect it will also impede understanding of one's own religion. In the parochial center of learning, the significance of the opinion or perspective on the external environment, although one can hardly claim to ignore or exclude it, cannot be so decisive as the opinion and perspective on the tradition itself.

From the university perspective on "reality," it is impossible to locate "the Jewish people"; what comes into view are only various groups called "Jewish," a term bearing various meanings in diverse settings and serving particular functions within different societies. Thus, to one outside the tradition, the "Jews" as a group are best defined functionally and episodically. In the Jewish school, on the other hand, "the Jewish people" loses its quotation marks. From his own viewpoint the believing Jew cannot deny the reality of Jewish history. Indeed, in Jewish schools the Jewish people constitutes a central category of analysis, on a par with Jewish Law, the God of Abraham, Isaac, and Jacob, or the hope for the end of days and the advent of the Messiah. Thus Jewish history represents a vital field of study in Jewish seminaries, for in that context peoplehood as a construct serves to unify the otherwise discrete and disparate data concerning the Jews. Jewish history provides a chief source for the verification and validation of theological or ideological convictions in an institution so defined. The appeal to the past, together with the recognition of the authority of some men in it, is the presupposition of religious thought for those who are Jewish by identity.

Judaism Within the History of Religions

What is the role of Jewish studies in the history of religions? The techniques of the history of religions and its categories of analysis have been applied unflinchingly, mostly by scholars of Christian descent, to every religious tradition of mankind, both archaic and modern, except for two, Christianity and Judaism. Of the two,

Judaism is still less studied than Christianity. To be sure, the Scriptures of ancient Israel have undergone religious-historical study, and the Jewish sectarian environment between the Maccabees and the first century A.D. (including the early Church) has been carefully examined from many perspectives. Yet practically no work has been done, except by a very few individuals, on the history of Judaism since that time. No subdivision within the history of religions known as "history of Judaism" has yet come into existence. The reason is that, for Christianity, "history of religions" was really meant to provide a means of studying the religions of the Orient. The history of Judaism was clearly to be subsumed within the "Judaeo-Christian tradition," which for theological reasons was not to be subjected to the same kind of analyses. The "Judaeo" part of the Judaeo-Christian tradition, according to this conception, usually drops away about A.D. 70, but never later than A.D. 135. Similarly, in Protestant and nonsectarian schools, the "Roman Catholic" part of the "Western" Christian tradition (or, under secular auspices, "civilization") ends at the Reformation. Such extraordinary events in the history of Roman Catholicism as the nineteenth-century Renaissance somehow find little, if any, place in histories of Western "Judaeo-Christianity."

The truth is that the university has been basically *Protestant*—though nonsectarian, liberal, and kindly disposed toward Jewish and Catholic as well as Hindu, Buddhist, and Moslem students and their religions. It was the Protestant vision which determined American university perspectives until the most recent past. That vision is, admittedly, broader and more mature than the Jewish or Roman Catholic equivalents. The New Testament and the history of Christianity are not systematically studied in any Jewish-sponsored university, in this country or in the State of Israel, except in relationship to the history of Judaism, whereas great attention has been paid at notable nonsectarian, Protestant-oriented universities to the Jewish tradition. Philip Ashby points out that the history of the history of religions in America cannot be separated from the history of Protestant theological education.[5] I think one may fairly add that the history of all forms of the study of religion in secular American universities can be written in terms of the history of cultural, if not religious, Protestantism. Nevertheless, it is hard to see how others, of different religious traditions or of secular orientation, have improved upon the Protestant record.

With the growing maturity of the history of religions, however, I see no alternative to both the inclusion of Jewish data in that discipline and the application of the issues and methods of that discipline to the study of Judaism. These, I suggest, are the specific points at which Jewish studies have their most promising, best-integrated place within the university (outside of Near Eastern studies).

The history of religions, as I understand it, focuses upon the phenomena and the morphology of religions. It raises questions concerning the interpretation of the religious structures, including myths, ideas, theological attitudes, and rites and rituals, as means of perceiving reality, or organizing it, or construing it, used by men in diverse circumstances. The history of Judaism has already contributed considerable data to that inquiry, mainly through the researches, in our own day, of Erwin R. Goodenough and Gershom G. Scholem, each of whom has shown, the one with archaeological, the other with mystical sources, the possibilities of relating Jewish religious data to the broader patterns discerned in other religious materials. Goodenough was, and Scholem is, primarily a historian of religion, secondarily a historian of Judaism—though this ordering of interests affected not so much the result as the attitude, motivation, and focus of concern. Yet, although Goodenough and Scholem have contributed much, we are only just beginning to appreciate the potential uses to be made of Jewish data. When one considers, for example, that there is still no study of phenomenology of the rabbi, in his inseparable political, cultural, and religious roles, one wonders how the nature of religious leadership can as yet be fully and properly comprehended. The rabbi, no less than the shaman, ought to provide basic information about the nature of the religious virtuoso and what he represents to the minds of his followers.

More broadly, however, one may suppose that Judaism, which seems so remote and intellectual in its central value structure, is among the religions which have in past times laid the greatest stress upon the man-God in various forms, not only rabbinical but also Messianic and, certainly within Hassidism, mediatorial. In its struggle against modern Christianity, modern Judaism has insisted that Jesus "could not possibly have been accepted by normative Jews as the Messiah" because the Jews could not have believed in a man-God or in a spiritual Savior who was not a politician or a general. That denial, if correct, required the exclusion of Hassidism, only two generations behind the German Jewish scholars, of Frankism, three generations, and of Sabbateanism, four generations earlier. But it also excluded the possibility of comprehending the figure of the Talmudic rabbi himself.

A second interesting theme is surely the transmutation of religion with the desuetude of the ancient ways of perceiving reality. Descriptions of archaic or so-called primitive religions normally omit reference to modern or contemporary religious phenomena except among still archaic peoples. But the great question in the history (not merely philosophy) of religion must be: What happens when archaic reality comes to an end and modernism begins? It is one thing to regret, condemn, look back fondly or sadly. It is quite another simply to ignore the fact that something called, and calling itself, *religion* has persisted into modern times in various ways and forms and therefore requires study. I can think of no more interesting example of a religion in the throes of transmutation into the modern idiom, better documented, with more variations in time and space and subtleties of definition, than the history of modern Judaism.[6] I have mentioned only two issues within the history of religions which cannot, I think, be satisfactorily discussed without considerable attention to the history of Judaism. There are many others.

It is therefore the history of *Judaism* which finds a most natural accommodation within the university curriculum. As a set of structures to be analyzed, and not as a set of theological (or other) propositions to be evaluated, Judaism becomes interesting in that setting. It is self-evident that the same principle holds for all religions, including Christianity. In particular, like the theologies of other traditions, the study of Jewish theology, *except* when examined from a comparative or morphological perspective by historians of religion, and *not* as a self-validating system, has no place in the university curriculum. It is where Judaism, among other religious traditions, provides evidence of a particularity in which broader categories or issues may be exemplified, or find expression, that Judaism becomes relevant to the curriculum of the university. I think it likely that Judaism will make its contribution toward the definition of larger structures of analysis. Eliade's work on archaic religions, Hinduism, and Christianity quite naturally provided him with particular data, out of which generalities or categories of analysis emerged. Given somewhat different data—a religion mostly without cathedral or temple for thousands of years, for example— he might well have raised different issues to begin with. Judaism focuses, in the terms of analysis proposed by Professor Jonathan Z. Smith, upon the following structures: holy people, the structure of election; Holy Land, the structure of sacred space, Zion and exile, Temple and synagogue; holy days, the structure of sacred time, the Sabbath, the feasts, the daily service; holy rites, structures of initiation; holy law and holy book, the cosmic law, personal piety, the law and interpretation; holy men, rabbi and student, the philosopher, the magician, the mystic, the Messiah, and the Hasid. These structures illustrate the viability of Eliade's basic scheme of analysis, but they also suggest ways in which particular Jewish data might modulate those categories.

I look forward, too, to the revivification of comparative studies of religions. In this the history of Judaism will both benefit and contribute. For example, taken in isolation, the rabbinical academy may be studied from antiquity to the present day, but without a significant awareness of what it really was, or what gave it its particular shape and method at a given time or place. When, however, one asks how the rabbinical school compared to the Hellenistic academy or to the Christian monastery, how it functioned in society and in the faith, as contrasted with the equivalent structures in Manichaeism, Buddhism or Islam, much new insight may result. And it was the rabbinical academy which was the apparently unique leadership-training institution of Judaism. Similarly, the comparison of the rabbi and the mandarin has yet to be undertaken. How much other central institutions, structures of belief or ritual or myth, and the like may be illumined by contrast or comparison with those of other religious traditions, we may only surmise. So while the history of Judaism has much to contribute to the history of religions, the issues of the wider field may raise wholly new questions, and provide quite novel perspectives, for the narrower one. Indeed, the richness of Scholem's perspectives derives in the end not from his grand study of Kabbalah, the science of which he himself founded, but rather from his ability to ask broader questions concerning the structure of Kabbalistic experience and thought.

We may turn, finally, to some issues confronting any aspect of the history of religions. First, what is to be the relationship between the historian of Judaism and the historian of religions? It is not unreasonable to expect the former to become familiar with the methods, issues, and ideas of the field as a whole and to see his task as part of a larger undertaking. But the other side of the coin is this: can a historian of religions make use of the history of Judaism without first becoming a specialist in Judaism? It is a painful and difficult question, for if, as I suggested above, Jewish studies must now depend to a significant extent upon the resources of Jewish, and not university, curricula, then how can a non-Jew hope to make a contribution to the history of Judaism or, through the history of Judaism, to the history of religions? On the one hand, it is difficult to conceive that anyone could acquire a genuine mastery of Judaism without a close study of the texts which for the most part preserve it. Judaism has few monuments outside of books, and the "native speakers" of the tradition, those who embody one or another aspect of the tradition in their own lives, are with few exceptions either not interested in addressing themselves to those outside the limited community of the faithful or incapable of doing so. Hence texts, almost alone, constitute the available evidence. To read them, one must know Hebrew and know it well. And to read them well, one must have undergone a long apprenticeship in mastering texts which represent a fundamentally *oral* tradition that has been transcribed.

Talmudic studies in particular cannot be mastered without a teacher or, better, several teachers in both the old and modern manners.

Can Judaism be studied by one who has no personal relationship to it? I think so. Many useful inquiries can be made by the historian of religions. First, since most of the major rabbinic texts of classical times exist in good English translations, the scholar who comes with particular issues or questions in mind may well locate what he feels is relevant and proceed to restudy the classical text in the original. Second, and more important, the historian of religions should be able to depend upon the results of the scholarship of others—philologists, text critics, commentators, historians, historians of law, art, music, and theology, sociologists, and other scientists—and not have to repeat the processes which originally yielded their results. In every field of intellectual endeavor one customarily depends in some measure upon others, either predecessors or colleagues in cognate fields. Jewish learning does not present an arcane and remote exception. The contrary view, that the true scholar is only one who has gone through the traditional processes of learning in the traditional modes and then rejected them for modern scholarship, predominates in many circles of Jewish scholarship. It reveals the latent mandarinism of Jewish learning (itself a datum for the history of religions). The mastery of specific texts, mastered in ancient ways, through the old commentaries upon the old questions, constitute the primary qualification for scholarship. What is important is not what one can do with what one knows, but what one has "been through," as if exposure to the texts magically transformed and therefore qualified the student. Modern scholarship adds a second qualification, namely, disenchantment with the old methods after such exposure to them. It is no less a magical view of learning, but one which elevates to a norm the experience of alienation.

The question of studying a religion not one's own generally depends upon the supposition that one's own religion plays a central part in one's capacity to comprehend some other. I do not see this as a serious classroom problem at the outset. Professor Jonathan Smith's syllabus opens with the words: "In this course, we will survey some of the basic religious structures of Judaism, using categories

derived from the discipline of the History of Religions. Your task
will be to try to interpret a representative sample of Jewish religious
expressions—not in order to judge them as 'true' or 'false,' or to ask
questions as to their contemporary or personal 'relevance'—but
rather to strive to understand what they have meant and mean to
a group who have expressed themselves, and the meaning of their
existence, who have constructed and interpreted their world and
their history through these religious myths, symbols, and rituals."
In my view, that sentence partially lays to rest the ghost of "personal
involvement." (But see below.)

This is not to say that the study of the history of Judaism is not
likely to raise certain broader questions about the nature of religion or the "science" of religion. After the tasks of description,
interpretation, and understanding have been undertaken, the further
responsibility of reconstituting the data into the raw material for
philosophy of religion has yet to be carried out. But I do not see
how that work can be done in the narrow framework of the history
of Judaism, as it is studied in the university classroom. Rather, it is
to be done in two ways and for two different purposes: first, in the
Jewish seminary, for theological purposes; and, second, in the
philosophy of religion, for phenomenological purposes.

One can hardly overestimate, moreover, the importance *for* Jewish learning of the study of the history of Judaism within the context of the history of religions. Ashby quotes Kitagawa as follows:

> The expert in one religion must also be cognizant of the nature,
> history, and expressions of religion beyond the one religion he seeks
> to understand. Adequate understanding of one religion is seldom,
> if ever, achieved by knowledge about that religion only. The his-
> torian of religions needs to possess wide knowledge of his subject in
> its universal expressions if he is to fathom one religion in depth.[7]

So far, with the major exceptions of Scholem and Goodenough, historians of Judaism have not taken comparative approaches very
seriously. It is true that they have conjectured about "influences" of
one thing upon something else—for example, Iranian influences
upon Qumran; but only rarely have they transcended such narrow,
positivistic questions.

Most scholars of Jewish subjects would, moreover, accept Kitagawa's statement if it were phrased in any terms other than religion. It is recognized that one must have command of several languages, literatures, histories, and cultures in order to study various aspects of the Jews or Judaica. Jewish scholarship was born in the age of positivism, however, and has remained ever since the last refuge of fundamentalist, naive, positivistic thinking. It has, therefore, not even bothered to apply its reductionist presuppositions to Judaism as a religion but, instead, has by and large ignored it from the start. So very little effort is devoted to the study of the history of Judaism that it is not even included in the curriculum of the Jewish Theological Seminary or in the programs of most other institutions of Jewish learning. If it were possible, some scholars of Judaica would deny that Judaism has existed as a religion in any sense, regarding it only as a law, a culture or "civilization," a nation (people), or something—anything—other than a "religion," or religious tradition. Others will go so far as to deny that Judaism, if it is a religion, has had any theologies. An examination of the pages of Jewish scholarly journals will uncover remarkably few articles about Jewish religion, though there are a great many which contribute in some way to the study of Jewish religion. But those contributions take the form of intellectual or social history, philology, sociology, and textual criticism. The central contribution to the study of Judaism now emerging in the universities will be a methodology appropriate to the study of the history of Judaism joined with concern for that study.

We therefore have a provisional task at hand: to learn what are appropriate issues and methods and to bring these issues and methods to bear upon a rich and practically untouched, almost unknown religion. Since that religion has entered a new age in its history, with the general decay of pre-modern forms in the West, it should be clear that few Jews are in the situation of the Buddhist who comes to the West to study Buddhism. Similarly, since the effort to convert the Jews seems finally to be concluded, except as an eschatological hope to be left for the eschaton, Christians normally do not come to the study of Judaism in order to master the information necessary to undertake a mission to the Jews. Normally atheists are less bothered by the absurdities of Judaism than by those of Christianity, which impinge more readily upon their consciousness. One's personal emotional condition can play no role of consequence in the study of a religion which few in the West have held in its classical forms for at least a century. Accordingly, whatever engagement of feeling we find may be of two kinds. First, it may be similar to the engagement of the classicist or the antiquarian, namely, a fondness for the dead past and its glories. Since it is dead, one may speak of its glories. So far as it is alive—and in its many modulations Judaism is very much alive—one cannot yet know what these glories may be, or what they are not. But the history of Judaism extends backward in time far, far beyond the nineteenth century, to at least the destruction of the first Temple, and I see sufficient grounds for many far-reaching investigations long before "feelings" and "involvements" pose much difficulty. Since Eliade refers to problems of aesthetics, it may be useful to draw an analogy from the study of the history of art. One may penetrate very deeply, I think, into the art of Rembrandt without for a single minute intending to paint in his fashion. One may similarly penetrate deeply into the understanding of Jewish religion on its own plane of reference, or on the plane of reference of religion as a phenomenon in human history, without intending to adopt that religion or any other. The "modernization" of Judaism, therefore, is what may make possible the study of its history.

Nonetheless, I think I err on the side of optimism. There is a second form of engagement of feeling not to be ignored or denied. The very involvement of Jewish scholars in the study of Judaism is bound to operate as a personal factor. The influence of Yehezkel Kaufman's *History of the Religion of Israel* upon biblical scholars of Conservative Jewish origin cannot be explained entirely in terms of the persuasiveness of Kaufman's case, if only because he has made very little headway elsewhere. Kaufman supplies, rather, a peculiarly satisfying way for biblical scholarship in a supposedly modern form to coexist with a very traditional, indeed primitive, formulation of Jewish theology, especially for people who want to continue to study the Bible as revelation. Having abandoned the classical faith in the Pentateuch as revealed by God to Moses on Mt. Sinai, the Conservative Jewish scholar finds comfort in Kaufman's arguments leading to much the same faith, but on a much more positivistic basis, in the "Mosaic revolution" of monotheism within Israelite culture. It would, moreover, be a misunderstanding of the modernization of Judaism to suppose that modern Jews see themselves as discontinuous with the past. On the contrary, the very stuff of their modernism is the effort to restructure or re-form inherited, archaic beliefs, attitudes, and patterns. Whether this is quite self-consciously undertaken, as in Reform and Conservative Judaism, or quite unself-conscious to begin with, as among so-called Orthodox and secular Jews, is not at issue here. What is important is that the modern proceeds from the archaic, and their relationships are subtle and difficult to comprehend. Hence the Jewish scholar of Judaism, however secular or objective he may think himself, must still conscientiously attempt to meet Kitagawa's conditions, just as other historians of religion must, and for much the same reason: "First is a sympathetic understanding of religions other than one's own; second is an attitude of self-criticism, or even skepticism, about one's own religious background. And third is the 'scientific' temper." [8] In the beginning the Jewish historian of Judaism must see both himself and his enterprise as themselves constituting data in the modern history of Judaism. So, as elsewhere, the very act of scholarship affects what is under study.

Conclusion

The broad range of Jewish studies may contribute to the university curriculum at many points, but the particular point at which a specialist in Jewish studies most nearly approximates the university's needs is in the field of the history of Judaism. This is not to suggest that specialists in the Hebrew language and the study of Hebrew literature do not belong in departments of Near Eastern languages and literatures, for they do, even though before recent times Hebrew literature was hardly a Near Eastern creation at any single, significant stage in its history after the tenth century. Specialists in the sociology of the Jewish community may well make a note-worthy contribution to the social sciences. Specialists in a given period and locale of Jewish history obviously have their appropriate place in a history department, so long as they are adequately trained to make a contribution to the broader interests of that department. Specialists in medieval Jewish philosophy or in modern Jewish "thought" may join in the discussions of the history of philosophy, or even in modern philosophical discourse pursued in old-fashioned ways (where these still persist). But so far as Jewish studies cover an *area* by means of many *disciplines,* there can be no place for a department of Jewish studies, though a center involving disciplinary specialists of many kinds obviously would serve a useful purpose. And so far as a university offers a strong program in the study of religions, it is in *that* program that its primary appointment in Jewish studies should quite naturally find its place, but not to the exclusion of an appointment in Hebrew language and literature. Given the predominant content of those studies, I think this is the only appropriate way of handling the matter.

There is one final point to be made: the development of Jewish studies in universities must not be shaped to meet the parochial interests of the Jewish community, the synagogue, or Judaism. Jewish community groups in recent times have discovered that the future of the community is being decided upon the campus. They have therefore chosen to strengthen programs aimed at influencing the Jewish college student to come to an affirmative decision upon basic issues of Jewish identity and commitment. As chaplaincy, or Hillel programs, such efforts are wholly unobjectionable. It is, however, quite natural for Jewish community groups to look upon professors in the field of Jewish learning in general, and of the history of Judaism in particular, as allies in the "struggle." They are widely expected to continue in the classroom the advocacy of Judaism which begins in the synagogue schools and continues in the pulpit. Secular Jewish organizations, interested in recruiting future leaders for their fund-raising and other programs, similarly turn to the campus and therefore to the professor of Jewish studies, particularly when he is a Jew to begin with, for support. Jewish studies certainly belong in parochial settings as well as in universities. When in universities, however, neither such studies nor those responsible for pursuing them must be used for propagandistic purposes of any kind. It is not the duty of the professor of the history of Judaism, or of Hebrew, to interest himself in the state of the souls of his students, whether Jewish or gentile. It will render his true task impossible if he does so, except insofar as he sees himself, and his students, as themselves constituting data for the study of the history of Judaism. It is certainly not the task of any professor to serve other than university commitments. It may, therefore, be wise for universities to avoid dependence upon Jewish community funds in the creation and maintenance of programs in the field of Jewish learning. I am not suggesting that the Jewish community and synagogue are more dangerous as a pressure group than any other, but only that they are no less so. In any event, rabbis and others who have achieved considerable mastery of Jewish traditional learning are not on that account appropriate candidates for full or, more especially, part-time university posts, any more than are local priests or ministers. Nothing will so endanger the healthy development of Jewish learning in its various modes within the university as the exploitation of that development for other than strictly and narrowly defined university purposes.

Judaic studies, that is, the study of the history of Judaism, and Hebrew studies, the study of Hebrew language and literature, together belong within the university curriculum of the humanities, the latter to serve the interests not only of linguists or Semitists but also of students of religion. If, as G. E. von Grunebaum said, "A humanistic education will essay to evoke the widest possible range of responses to the stimuli of civilization," [9] then within it the history of Judaism provides a number of important perspectives. It is the account of the development of a world religion from almost the very beginnings of human history up to the present day. Its history includes the most varied forms and expressions of that world religion, its organization into several sorts of political systems, its narrowing into essentially salvific forms, its broadening into a whole civilization (in Central and Eastern Europe); and then its renewed development in a series of complex and subtle responses to the modern situation. In the development of Judaism, foreign cultural traditions were absorbed, modified, eliminated, illustrating the processes of cultural interaction and transformation.[10] Finally, the history of Judaism contains a number of unifying elements, shared by other Western religions yet in some ways quite unique. Judaism is, as von Grunebaum said of Islam, "both close enough to the Western view of the world to be intellectually and emotionally understandable and sufficiently far removed from it to deepen, by contrast, the self-interpretation of the West." [11]

COMMENT

The primary weakness of this paper is in what it does not pretend to treat, and that is, the study of Hebrew literature in Departments of Near Eastern Studies (under their several names). And that omission is not minor, for it signals a major lacuna in the author's comprehension of the study of Judaism, namely, the importance, to that study, of literary criticism, in particular of modern Hebrew literature, on the one side, and of studies of fiction by and about Jews and on Jewish topics, on the other. It is only recently that I have become aware of how much is to be learned about Jewish religion from the literary study of literature, of its structures and modes of symbolic expression, as much as of its themes. Clearly, Jews addressing themselves to non-Jewish problems teach us much about the Jews, including the imaginative reconstruction of reality we call religion. I take for granted that included in the study of Judaism are subjects not normally understood as contributing to the inquiry into the nature and definition of religions, for example, Zionism and other modes of Jewish nationalism, the development of Jewish Socialism, Yiddish literature, and similar subjects obviously closely related to and expressive of Judaism. But what is important about poetry and fiction?

The less important aspect of poetry and fiction is the self-conscious "Jewish message" therein contained. This tends to be shrill and homiletical, for instance, in Fierberg's Whither? *which pretends to capture and symbolize the dilemma of the modern Jew. On the other hand, as Professor Arnold Band has shown, what is regarded as folk-tale and folk-literature turns out, upon closer examination, to reveal the presence of literary conventions of a highly complex and subtle character, to convey meanings, through deftness of organization and expression, accessible only to extraordinarily sensitive people. Band has moreover shown that the Hasidic tale testifies to artistic sophistication of an exceptional height in East European Judaism. The Hasidic story is so carefully structured as to convey meanings on many levels, exhibits such a complexity of symbolic expression as to testify to remarkably sensitive audiences. When we fully grasp the symbolic structures and metaphysical meanings of these stories, we shall have a much richer understanding of classical Judaism than we have at this time.*

A second point that should have been made in this paper flows from the first. Our entire definition of the data of modern Judaism has been impoverished. We have tended to concentrate all too much upon the study of philosophers of Judaism, chiefly those in Germany and America, with the notion that they teach us what is modern about Modern Judaism. With noteworthy exceptions, however, the closer we come to the modern thinkers, the more clearly we perceive the shallowness of their grasp of the classical sources of Judaism. Not uncommonly, they exhibit an appreciation at best of biblical literature, as though classical Judaism and the Tanakh were more or less the same thing. By contrast, the ways in which the various modes and expressions of traditionalism in the nineteenth and twentieth centuries constitute responses to the modern condition have been scarcely examined, let alone appreciated. The development of the mighty yeshiva-system of Eastern Europe is the work of the nineteenth century. The organization of traditionalism into Orthodoxy is the effect of response to challenges of modernity. Still more interesting, the nineteenth and twentieth centuries witnessed the renaissance of the exegetical work on classical Rabbinic literature, particularly Mishnah, Tosefta, Palestinian Talmud, and the like, and the greater part of this work was accomplished in East European settings or by scholars educated in them but working in the Land (later, State) of Israel or in America, Britain, and

Germany. In fact some of the most daring and original work done from the time of Maimonides was carried out in this very period. None of this is even hinted at in the foregoing paper, whose definition, therefore, of the problematic of the study of Judaism in modern times ("Modern Judaism") is vastly impoverished and flawed.

Critics of this paper, however, responded chiefly to the point, which the author thought obvious and scarcely worth stating (if not trivial), that "Jewish history" is not a viable academic subject, because it constitutes a theological, not an academic, category of inquiry. I was astonished at the negative response to this point, even though I understood it and was not wholly unsympathetic. For in pointing out that "the Jewish people" which stands behind and defines "Jewish history" constitutes a theological category, not obviously-verified by the this-worldly data of Jews in various settings and cultures, I met head-on that positivistic anti-religious trait of mind characteristic of Jewish scholars working in Jewish schools. I do not regard the statement in the foregoing paper as adequate, therefore, to the issue. When asked to address myself to the problem in relationship to a recent book on the subject, I took the occasion to expand the framework of my discussion. That paper appears in History and Theory, August, 1975.

FOOTNOTES

1. For a survey of the existing pattern, see Arnold J. Band, "Jewish Studies in American Liberal Arts Colleges and Universities," in *American Jewish Year Book*, LXVII, ed. Morris Fine, Milton Himmelfarb, and Martha Jelenko (New York and Philadelphia: Jewish Publication Society of America, 1966), 3-30. Band compiled a list of 54 professors and 34 Hillel directors teaching courses at 92 American colleges and universities. Among the top graduate and undergraduate schools (41), Band found that what he calls "Judaics" are offered in the following departments:

   Near Eastern studies (including Oriental studies, etc.)—14
   Religious studies—12
   Classics—4
   Foreign languages (including modern languages, linguistics)—5
   German—2
   Jewish studies (or Hebrew studies)—2
   English—1
   Philosophy and religious studies—1

   The field seems mostly divided between departments of Near Eastern or Oriental studies, which stress language and literature, and departments of religion.

2. See the very helpful comments of Raphael Loewe, "Defining Judaism: Some Ground-clearing," *Jewish Journal of Sociology* VII/2 (1965), 153-175.

3. I am well aware that one- and multi-volume histories of the Jews have been written. These are invariably highly theological (ideological), frequently homiletical treatises, in which given themes, such as the nobility of the Jews and the heartlessness of their (generally) Christian neighbors, the literary productivity ("culture") of the Jews and the benighted and narrow minds of their neighbors, and the like, are played upon. Before World War II such histories concluded at the climax of "the Enlightenment and Emancipation," which seemed then to be the happy ending of the long bloody story. Afterward, the State of Israel generally provided the dramatic conclusion for the narrative. I know of only one exception to the rule that a comprehensive "history of the Jews" is bound to be of less than professional historical quality, and that is Salo W. Baron's *Social and Religious History of the Jews,* 15 vols. (New York: Columbia University Press, 1952).

4. Of special interest in this connection are N. N. Glatzer, "Beginnings of Modern Jewish Studies," in *Studies in Nineteenth-Century Jewish Intellectual History,* ed. A. Altmann (Cambridge: Harvard University Press, 1964), 27-45, and N. N. Glatzer, "Challenge to the Scholar: A Judaic View," in *Judaism* XI/3 (1962), 210-220. I subscribe wholeheartedly to Professor Glatzer's theses in the latter article.

5. "The History of Religions," in *Religion,* ed. Paul Ramsey (Englewood Cliffs, N.J.: Prentice-Hall, 1965), 1-49, *passim.*

6. I have tried to present one useful structure of interpretation of the history of modern Judaism in "From Theology to Ideology: The Transmutations of Judaism in Modern Times," in *Churches and States,* ed. K. H. Silvert, (New York: American Universities Field Staff, 1967), 13-48.

7. "The History of Religions," 44.

8. "The History of Religions in America," in *The History of Religions: Essays in Methodology,* ed. Mircea Eliade and Joseph M. Kitagawa (Chicago: University of Chicago Press, 1959), 1-30. Quotation is on 15.

9. G. E. von Grunebaum, "Islam in a Humanistic Education," in *The Traditional Near East,* ed. J. Stewart-Robinson (Englewood Cliffs, N.J.: Prentice-Hall, 1966), 36-68 (reprinted from *The Journal of General Education* IV [1949], 12-31). Quotation is on 36.

10. Paraphrase of von Grunebaum, *ibid.,* 37.

11. *Ibid.*

Part Four

EDUCATIONAL ISSUES

EDUCATIONAL ISSUES

Introduction

Having the privilege of participating in the education of future scholars and teachers for American (and, in one case, Israeli) universities, I devote the larger part of my energies to the nurture and needs of graduate students. At the outset of the program inaugurated upon my coming to Brown University in 1968, I prepared a paper explaining my conception of what was to be done. This involved two questions, first, a picture of the scholarly problems to be taken up, second, an account of the educational programs to be effected. All this was offered in the setting of the work done at Brown, to be sure, but it was meant to present for critical discussion one theory of graduate education. Since that time, I have not seen discussion of alternate theories, either offered in criticism of the way our group has defined its work, or in the constructive effort to explain how other aspects of scholarship in Jewish areas were to be organized.

It is disappointing to observe how little theoretical writing, or other discussion, on graduate education has been forthcoming. It is not, after all, as if we have attained a consensus, let alone certainty of the correctness of our theory of the work. Our program at Brown is under continuing criticism on the part of those who bear primary responsibility for it, criticism founded upon the concrete results of the program, the failures and successes of the individual students who pass through it. Nonetheless, the main lines laid out in 1968 and presented to colleagues both at the first meeting of the Association of Jewish Studies and at the American Academy of Religion remain pretty much as they were at the outset.

Much has changed, as our faculty has grown, and as I have come to appreciate how much is to be learned from professors in our department who work with different methods from my own and on different religions from Judaism.

The two scholarly conferences at which this paper was presented, to be sure, allowed for no discussion, and no other conference centered upon the issues, both scholarly and educational, raised here. The one conference in which graduate education was discussed concentrated on bemoaning the failures of programs not in "Jewish studies" producing scholars for positions in that area. While curricular developments in various centers of higher learning were described, none was presented within a theory of scholarship or of the requirements of a specific discipline within the larger area. The absence of a clear polemic in these papers, directed in particular toward developments within the intellectual world of Jewish learning, is on account of the paucity of serious discourse on that subject.

VII

GRADUATE EDUCATION IN JUDAICA: PROBLEMS
AND PROSPECTS

I

Educators responsible for graduate programs in whatever the discipline or field share a number of common problems in defining and carrying out their task.[1] Although I shall concentrate on one aspect of a relatively modest field, namely, the graduate study of Judaism within the science of religion, I hope these specific observations will contribute to more general insight into the current situation.

First, however, comes the problem facing everyone: the demand for relevance. In the study of Judaism as elsewhere, graduate students insist that their studies be relevant, although often they are not clear about what these studies should be relevant *to*. Indeed, relevance means pretty much what you want: rejection of discipline in favor of subjectivity; expectation of immediate achievement and instant wisdom; assertion of egalitarianism over the aristocracy of knowledge; imposition of opinion in place of, indeed in preference to, fact. Guided by mere impressions, we suppose everything is new. I suspect that the resentment voiced in demands for relevance is far older than its new vocabulary. It represents a reaction to the age-old demands of rigorous scholarship. What, after all, does scholarship require, if not discipline, patience, respect for the knowledge and insight of others, suspicion of generalizations, and reverence for facts? The existential realities actually have not changed much. We demand, first of all from ourselves, but also from our students, hard, sustained work; critical thought; and, above all, mature judgment.

127

Yet how many in any generation are capable of attaining these? We expect severe, albeit pointed and impersonal, criticism, rational commitment to disciplined learning, abdication of self in the interest of truth, and submission of opinion in the court of learning. How many in any age have had the maturity of character and the dedication to learning to endure these rewarding trials?

Scholarship is a function of character and personality as much as it is a product of memory, learning, patience, and hard work. A daring and courageous person creates daring and courageous theses. A patient and devoted mind produces immaculate and abiding results. A constructive and amiable master raises up self-confident disciples for the coming generation. Those lacking in confidence or intelligence are always available to destroy and denigrate the best efforts of mature men. Above all, a critical and discerning intellect invariably serves to purify and elevate the ideas of easily-satisfied careerists.

We cannot define a Judaica Ph.D. out of context. In general, the Ph.D. represents as much variety as the universities that grant it and scholars that take it. In my view, the Ph.D. marks a stage in one's development. It serves as a professional degree, not as a certification of virtue or of a perfected and completed, thus ended, education. The function of the Ph.D. program, therefore, needs to be spelled out carefully in its specific settings. Generally such a program should educate men to continue their own education, to supervise that of others, and to pursue consequential inquiries in specific disciplines. The Ph.D. degree, as distinguished from the function of programs leading to it, obviously serves to certify college teachers— but what it certifies *about* them is that they have satisfactorily completed a program. Certainly the degree (apart from the program) serves other purposes, but these do not require specification here. When Freud was asked, "What must a person be able to do to be considered normal?" he replied, "lieben und arbeiten," to love and to work. What must a person be able to *do* when he has completed a Ph.D. program and holds the degree? He must be able to read critically, to write accurately, to teach cogently, and to advance knowledge. Many Doctors of Philosophy are thus qualified, though not all who are granted the title deserve it.

II

Although no form of graduate education in the United States is very old—the first graduate schools were founded at Harvard in 1872 and Johns Hopkins in 1876, less than a century ago—both undergraduate and graduate studies in the field of Judaica are even more recent. Aspects of Judaic studies—"the discipline which deals with the historical experiences, in the intellectual, religious, and social spheres, of the Jewish people in all centuries and countries" —were touched on from earliest times. The study of the Hebrew language and Hebrew Scriptures is not new in American higher education, although the context has not always been Judaica. Today, moreover, many disciplines in the social sciences and the humanities pursue aspects of Judaica. Professors of Anthropology, Sociology, Psychology, not to mention Politics, Philosophy, History, Comparative Literature, Near Eastern Studies, and History of Science—all make considerable contributions to Judaic learning.

Likewise, a graduate program leading to the Ph.D. in some phase of Judaic studies may be undertaken at Brandeis, Berkeley, Brown, U.C.L.A., Chicago, Columbia, Cornell, Dropsie, Harvard, Indiana, Iowa, Johns Hopkins, Michigan, New York University, Hunter, Pennsylvania, Princeton, Rutgers, Smith, Texas, Vanderbilt, Wayne, Wisconsin at Madison, and Yale. I need not mention the many schools, including the above, that also offer the Ph.D. in the study of the Bible. Many of these programs focus on Hebrew language and literature in the context of Semitics or Near Eastern studies in ancient, medieval, and modern times. Only a few concentrate on aspects of the history, religion, and culture of the Jews.

The picture is still more complicated by the development in Jewish schools of various sorts of doctoral programs, apart from studies leading to rabbinical ordination. These include programs at Hebrew Union College, Jewish Theological Seminary, and Yeshiva University. Colleges training teachers for the Jewish schools likewise grant doctorates.

The proliferation of all these different kinds of programs indeed is a new phenomenon. Arnold Band points out that 50 percent of the professors of Judaica in U.S. colleges and universities received their graduate training in the United States. Of these, Columbia, through Salo Baron, and Harvard, through Harry Wolfson, have made by far the largest contributions. The development of professional doctoral studies in Judaica cannot be dated much before the careers of Baron and Wolfson, who retired very recently. Hence the history of American and Canadian doctoral education in Judaica covers no more than half a century or, more accurately, one generation.

Definition of the field has barely begun. As Band observes, "It is almost impossible to tell what a man's specialty is unless one reads his publications or his doctoral thesis. The various areas of Jewish scholarship are so often undefined and interrelated that the terms used in academic titles or catalogue descriptions do not convey an exact meaning." The field is so primitive that processes of definition, differentiation, and specialization are still incomplete.

In the context of the science of religion, doctoral programs in Judaica exist at Columbia, Temple, and Brown universities. The first is well-established; the latter two were begun last year. In addition, graduate study of Judaism takes place in the Department of Near Eastern and Judaic Studies at Brandeis University and in various departments and programs at Yeshiva University, Jewish Theological Seminary, Dropsie College, and a few other places. Graduates of such programs, however, rarely have the opportunity to take courses in the study of religions. Approaching the teaching of Judaism in undergraduate programs, they suppose the primary requirement is "objectivity"! They have little, if any, notion of what their colleagues do and why. Because of this situation, if a Ph.D. program functions to prepare college teachers for various departments, then the increasing number of Judaica positions in departments of religious studies will have to be met by doctoral programs located in the graduate departments of *that* particular field.

III

Graduate education in Judaica in a department of religious studies aims at preparing teachers of Judaica *for such departments.* I must emphasize the modesty of this intention. Clearly, only some of the phenomena of Judaic studies find a place in the study of religions. When the disciplines of history of religions and theology, religious ethics, textual and literary criticism, social scientific studies of religions and philosophy of religion—the disciplines normally present among the faculty of a department of religious studies—come to bear upon Judaic data, scholars in such disciplines naturally select from the variety of data those best studied through their methods. Further, in this context the phenomena of Judaism, like those derived from other religious traditions, are not self-validating, of interest for their own sake. They are important because they exemplify something of interest to the historian of religion, theologian, social scientist, or philosopher of religion. One may criticize the methods and results of these disciplines, but so far as their methods are sound for any data, they are acceptable for Judaic ones as well.

Graduate Judaic education in a department of religious studies therefore should equip the young scholar with a method, or better still, a variety of methods, inquiries, and issues, which he may bring to bear upon the study of Judaism. The graduate student, furthermore, ought to have some insight into how these methods work elsewhere, on other sorts of material or on other religious traditions. He should have a considerable familiarity with the history of the study of religions, with the "theory of religion," and with comparative data. He should work both as an expert in comparative religious studies who concentrates on one body of data and as a master of a variety of research methods who applies these to studies of Judaism. The young doctor ought, moreover, to have a broad grasp of Judaism so that he can teach a variety of courses and, in his scholarly work, cite data from more than one country, period, or genre of literature. If his subject is religion, and within it, Judaism, he should be able either to make general observations on religion and on Judaism or

—a more reasonable requirement—to recognize the limitations of such observations.

He requires, furthermore, a particular scholarly field or problem. He needs to stand within a tradition of Judaic learning. Within the field of religious studies, Gershom Scholem created one such tradition, the study of Jewish mysticism. Harry A. Wolfson developed another, the study of Jewish philosophy. Others include studies of particular periods and documents or archaeological data, such as the religion of Israel in ancient times, or the nature of Judaism in late antiquity as it is revealed in talmudic and archaeological materials. Models for the tradition of studying religions in late antiquity are the late Arthur Darby Nock and my teacher Morton Smith. The tradition of textual commentary, rooted deep in the history of Judaism, has been enhanced recently by applying philological and form-critical methods. I point to Saul Lieberman and the late Y. N. Epstein as noteworthy masters of philological method. Form criticism and source criticism of Judaic literature are represented among the currently active generation by Abraham Weiss, Joseph Heinemann, and David Weiss. I offer these few instances to clarify what I mean by a "tradition" within a particular scholarly field.

My own ambition is to advance the historical study of talmudic and cognate literature in the context of the histories of the Jews and Judaism and of the history of religions in late antiquity. The two Talmuds have long been studied by lawyers and philologists, who have given us the advantage of an immense corpus of scholarship, both traditional and modern. Still incomplete is the study of Talmudic and other Judaisms of the period in which the Talmuds were created and to which they testify. We have, for example, no corpus of biographies of the great rabbis. We have no systematic accounts of the character of various rabbinical schools. We have few sophisticated and comparative studies of the theological and other religious notions of the rabbinical movement, or of particular authorities and generations. It is no criticism of the work of Schechter and Moore, Marmorstein, Buechler, and I. H. Weiss, Graetz, Yawitz and Halevy, Aaron Hyman and Y. S. Zuri, E. R. Goodenough, A. J. Heschel, and, among the living, Salo Baron, Samuel Belkin, and E. E. Urbach

—the list is not much longer—to observe that much remains to be done.

I believe that the study of rabbinical literature from late antiquity as well as of pertinent materials from other sources can be fruitfully pursued in departments of religious studies. Admittedly, not everything worthwhile in these data will be exhausted by scholarship under such auspices. Careful commentary on texts, translations, philological and related studies will always find important tasks. Their problems probably are solved best through disciplines other than those of religious studies, in departments of Semitics and Near Eastern languages, for one example, or in Jewish rabbinical seminaries, for another. But the study of rabbinic Judaism cannot fail to be enriched by the perspective of the study of religions generally and of religions in late antiquity in particular.

IV

These demands are easier to make than to meet. In planning particular programs of studies, the difficulties become acute. Moreover, each school must try to meet them in its own way, which will be determined to a large extent by its particular advantages and limitations. Here, accordingly, I do not think we can lay down general rules. Let me merely report how we have been trying to shape the new graduate program in *History of Religions: Judaism* at Brown. In line with what has already been said, our purposes are clearly to educate young scholars as teachers of Judaica in departments of religious studies, to enhance their knowledge both of related religious traditions and of the study of religions; to set them on scholarly projects in a particular tradition and concerning a particular body of data in a circumscribed place and period in the history of Judaism. Concentrating our best energies on this modest project, we hope to make a solid, albeit limited, contribution to Judaica.

Success in achieving our purposes is measured by two sets of examinations. The first, at the end of a year's study, concentrates on the comparative aspect and consists of papers in theory of religion, early Christianity, and theology. The second, preliminary to the dissertation, covers in varying ways the four conventional periods of the history of Judaism: biblical, talmudic, medieval, and modern. The papers concentrate of scholarly traditions, rather than on the reading of texts drawn from these periods. Students need to know the chief scholarly issues, the important scientific works, the central themes of the several periods. A further examination focuses upon preparation for the dissertation itself. The results ought to be broad knowledge of the field's scholarly enterprise and access to scholarship in cognate fields.

What advantages do we enjoy? (These, I think, are not ours alone.) First, considerable and preliminary preparation in languages and texts is necessary, and programs in Hebrew language and literature abound in this country. These do not invariably produce high level competence, but we can realistically decline admission to beginners in Hebrew and in rabbinic literature. We are able to set as a standard for admission some familiarity with rabbinic documents.

Furthermore, we are fortunately located near other universities offering complementary studies. Our graduate students may pursue, for example, readings in medieval Judaism in consultation with Professor Alexander Altmann at Brandeis University. We are able to invite specialists in fields not represented on our modest faculty to serve as examiners, on dissertation committees, and as counselors. Indeed, we are able to specialize precisely because substantial scholarly resources are nearby. In time to come, I hope a consortium may take shape, so that students registered in a graduate program anywhere in the field of Judaica may take courses or even enroll for an entire semester or year of study at other graduate schools offering subjects unavailable at home. If today there is no one place to study Judaica, that disability provides a splendid opportunity for each university to develop its particular interests and areas of specialization. Through cooperative arrangements, both formal and informal, we shall be able to turn the limitations of each university into advantages for the field as a whole.

We all benefit from the elaborate Judaica programs of Jewish seminaries and other institutions of higher Jewish learning. Students qualify for admission to graduate work in our department by acquiring elsewhere the rudiments of method, the necessary language skills and experience in reading texts. We are not equipped to teach these fundamental skills, but we must demand them. A college student aspiring to devote himself to Judaic studies today may begin work not in a graduate program such as the one I have described, but in an institution of higher Jewish learning in the United States or in the State of Israel. A "general education in Judaic studies," equivalent to the achievements of a major in English after high school and college years, may be attained in a few years of study, for example, at the Hebrew University. I encourage students if it is possible to go first to Jerusalem for a year or two, then to Brown, then back to Jerusalem or to an equivalent program in this country for further study. They can thereby acquire the broad and comprehensive learning we cannot provide. They bring us the insights and perspectives of colleagues elsewhere. If few undergraduates are now satisfactorily educated to undertake the kind of scholarship we envision, many opportunities exist for them to achieve the requisite breadth and depth.

V

Two classes of problems remain to be solved. First are those presented by the cultural environment. In all aspects of Judaica, not only in the ones mentioned earlier, we have a superfluity of experts. Every Jew who has read a book or two—and some who have not—considers himself not merely a primary datum in the history of Judaism, but also a significant authority. Everyone's opinion carries preponderant weight, it seems, and in particular every rabbi knows it all. Both we and our students need to insulate ourselves from the appeal of omniscience. We must re-enforce our commitment to specialization, therefore to competence in some few things. We must present a contrast: even among the things we need to know, we do not claim to be everywhere expert, but gladly rely on others and submit to their judgment and criticism.

A further environmental problem arises from several related opinions: First, the belief that without mastery, or at least considerable study, of the Babylonian Talmud in the classical mode, no one can do anything of importance in the Judaic field. A second view, related to this, considers studying the Talmud without much understanding meritorious in itself. Third, study of the Talmud can be done effectively only by the method of the classical yeshiva. Finally, the experience of alienation from the yeshiva's standards and conversion to those of modern historical scholarship is necessary for scientific work in Judaism. These beliefs together constitute a formidable obstacle for young men who have grown up in other than traditional Jewish schools and yet aspire to contribute to Judaic studies. The first is obviously false for the pre-talmudic period and, except in study of law and legal literature, probably false for the later periods as well. The second statement refutes itself. The third, that study of the Talmud can be done only in a classical yeshiva, cannot be settled by an argument. Sooner or later someone will settle it by making himself a first-rate Talmudist without going to a yeshiva, perhaps studying instead at the Hebrew University's excellent program. I see no reason why it cannot be done. If one does not have to go to a yeshiva to master the Talmud, then one need not be alienated to acquire the attitude of historical scholarship. In any event, beside the religious belief in the necessity of yeshiva training, much of the support for this position derives from the fact that so many great scholars of the past three or four generations followed this road. Then no thorough teaching of Talmud existed outside of Yeshivas, so, of course, it could not be mastered elsewhere. Now opportunities do exist.

This fact carries a special importance because of the tasks before us, tasks not yet completed by those who have conformed to the pattern held up to us not only as a religious ideal but as the exclusive means of preparation for Judaic scholarship. We do not have adequate translations of the corpus of rabbinical literature into European languages. We do not have a complete, scientifically consistent philological commentary for the Babylonian Talmud. We have not got even an incomplete and modest commentary of any sort for the whole of the Palestinian Talmud, which has never been properly translated. We do not yet have a complete concordance of either Talmud, nor of the greater part of midrashic literature. We do not even have critical texts for much of talmudic and cognate literature, nor even thorough compendia of variant readings for the whole corpus. We do not have a decent dictionary for rabbinical literature of late antiquity, certainly none providing up-to-date etymological studies. We do not have a thorough, detailed introduction to talmudic literature, one which carefully describes and dates each document and which summarizes and evaluates the manuscript evidence. We have no history or description of Talmudic law. These tasks could have been undertaken best by those made familiar with the sources by a classical education in a traditional Talmudic school. Yet, with respect and gratitude for what has been achieved by those who studied first in yeshivas, then in universities, I find no reason for excluding or intimidating other sorts of students. Much remains to be done, both by those with traditional and then critical, philological training, and by those with entirely other kinds of education. One does not have to denigrate the value of a particular educational pattern to show the viability of another. But it will *not* do to insist on education of one kind *only* for tasks which have not yet been achieved.

VI

Besides these environmental problems, which are beyond easy solution but lingering rather than critical, another set of difficulties result from the novelty of university Judaic studies. These can be solved, but they are critical.

First, we have no adequate source of fellowships, particularly for the peripatetic students I described. Too few universities provide graduate fellowships for foreign study, almost none have any for study in other universities in the United States. No consortium can develop without fellowship support, as yet unavailable.

Second, we have no satisfactory system for placement. A depart-

ment of religion may not be well-served by a Semitist, a department
of Near Eastern or oriental studies, by a historian of Judaism. The
differentiation of programs to clarify placement procedures remains
inadequate. Even the practical ways by which candidates make
themselves available and positions are made known are haphazard.
This problem faces many fields. In the study of Judaism in religion
departments it will probably be solved by the new Council on the
Study of Religion, organized by several organizations of religion
scholars under the auspices of the American Council of Learned
Societies.

Third, I am not persuaded that sufficient positions exist for the
growing number of prospective doctors. Growth in universities has
slowed, and new fields compete for limited budgets. Since rabbinical
seminaries generally prefer to employ their own doctors, and in any
event quite correctly impose conditions of conviction and religious
practice, those educated for university teaching and scholarship are
not invariably considered for Jewish institutional employment. Other
posts cannot be taken for granted. We must avoid making false
promises to young men and women considering careers in Judaica.

Fourth, we have not fully defined the range of scholarly tasks we
can undertake and satisfactorily carry out. We need a curriculum,
or, better yet, a set of curricula, appropriate to our field. The modest
program I described earlier has yet to take shape in a rational set of
courses, designed so that a person may learn in a few years all he
needs to know to do his job as it is here defined. Some other programs in Judaica do not aspire to even this much coherence and
cogency. Without differentiation or adequate specialization, Judaica
is so loosely defined that one may acquire a Judaic doctorate by
studying scarcely related subjects: e.g., biblical studies, medieval
mysticism, and American Jewish history.

Fifth, we lack above all a context for our individual studies. We
work too much alone. We tend not to read each other's books; we
work as autodidacts, approaching problems successfully solved by
others, or, more commonly, ignoring mistakes made by others. Each
scholarly book and article should come as an event for celebration.
We must rejoice in the achievements of colleagues, take pride in

them, find hope in their accomplishment. Books and articles of considerable sophistication and originality; meticulous translations; intelligent, comprehensive, and critical studies—must these be read only by the authors' friends and students? Can we not see ourselves as a fellowship of learning men, strengthened by one another, concerned for one another? Separately, after all, we do not add up to much. Together, we constitute a grand collegium, as the French reviewers refer to us: "The American Jewish school." Yet, if we are a school, where is our journal? Where do we find substantial and constructive critical reviews of serious books? Where do we even meet one another? These problems do not confront Judaica alone, still less only the study of the history of Judaism. They challenge graduate educators as a whole.

VII

I shall close on a personal note. When I taught at Dartmouth, much as I enjoyed undergraduates, I thought, "If only I could teach graduate students, then. . . ." Now at Brown I find undergraduate teaching a greater joy than ever, but graduate education looms up as an insurmountable mountain of difficulties, one more intimidating than the last. I find myself tempted to give up at the very outset, to concentrate solely on teaching undergraduates and perhaps graduates in other fields, and to pursue my own education and scholarly efforts. Perhaps in a little while I shall succumb to that temptation, but for the present I do not give up. The task, if difficult, is not unimportant. According to the effort is the reward. And, to quote R. Tarfon, to whom I devoted my earliest efforts, "The work is not yours to complete. But you are not free to desist from it."

COMMENT

One further point is called for by experience. Not only do we prepare young scholars for work in Departments of Religious Studies. We also prepare them for work in various sorts of Departments and in various kinds of colleges. This paper displays insufficient understanding of the varieties of the academic contexts and settings in which the work of education is carried out. While we must aim at a requisite level of erudition, to be exhibited by all doctoral students, we have also to make provision for the differing skills and predilections of young men and women. While all seek learning and hope to teach worthwhile and accurate information, some have greater ambition for teaching than for scholarship. Others have greater skills in the close reading and exegesis of texts, combined with substantial erudition, than in preparing balanced and judicious lectures, accounts of a whole problem or phenomenon. This paper lays too much stress upon the education of future scholars, insufficient emphasis upon that of future teachers. It falls therefore into the class of papers asking more of "Jewish studies" than other fields and areas of study ask of themselves. We owe our colleagues to do as good a job as anyone. We do not owe it to anyone to do better, nor do we have to do better, to find our rightful place in the university. Clearly, this is not an argument in defense of incompetence or ignorance. It is merely to say that the colleges and universities which turn to us for teachers and scholars are diverse, and we must respect their various commitments.

The noteworthy omission of this paper, therefore, is the topic of the preparation of future teachers, future colleagues, future counsellors and friends of students. I am inclined to doubt that courses in such ineffable and intangible topics can constitute more than exercises in vapidity and platitude. Yet within the graduate program, every student should have the opportunity first to work as a teaching assistant in a course with an experienced, and, hopefully, competent teacher, and second, should have the occasion in such a course to deliver his own lectures or to teach his own classes, under careful (but tolerant and benign) supervision. Colleges and universities can effectively focus the attention of graduate educators upon educational problems by asking whether candidates have had such experience, by inquiring about the specific, supervised classroom encounter available to candidates for appointment, and by giving preference to those self-evidently prepared actually to teach young people. Committees charged with seeking qualified professors (in this and in any other field) should request examples of courses candidates have taught or, at least, would teach if given the opportunity. They ought, further, to ask some of the larger questions pertinent to a given field or discipline, not merely sit patiently through half a chapter of a doctoral dissertation. Since many scholars publish very little, and most work is done by a handful, we merely face realities by laying stress upon teaching young doctors how to teach (and example is the best lesson) and even persuading them that teaching is noble and important.

In the five and a half years since this paper was written, little perceptible progress seems to have been made in solving the several problems outlined here. "Jewish studies" are still exactly that, undifferentiated and omnibus. Whatever a person's "specialization," he or she still represents himself or herself as qualified to teach just about everything. Colleges and universities continue to appoint people who claim greater breadth in this area of learning than anyone is apt to claim in any other. The careful specialization within the study of religions delineated here, while appreciated in some circles, remains exceptional. Fellowships deriving from extra-university funds still are few and indeed are awarded in a way quite out of phase with university calendars, leaving young people to wonder until the very last minute whether they will be able to continue their studies. Procedures of placement remain primitive. My caveat about the sufficiency of positions was excessively pessimistic in 1969; many people got jobs, more, indeed, than should have. But today no one can disagree. Too many young people are in too many graduate programs. Graduate curricula, leading to doctoral degrees, reveal more commonly no core or center than an integrated and logical pattern. The organization of the Association of Jewish Studies has made a measure of progress in bringing scholars into relation with one another. But its programmatic diversity underlines the conceptual chaos of the field as a whole, calling into question whether, indeed, we may speak of "Jewish studies" as a field at all. I remain persuaded, to be sure, that the work of graduate education must go forward, at least for a while, lest the coming generations be left without scholars worthy of both the quality of American colleges and universities at their best (and they are many and impressive) and the calling of the Jewish people and its tradition of learning.

A final point: The graduate program at Brown has undergone considerable modification, both formal and informal, in recognition of the resources of our own department. For example, as our program was enriched through the appointment of three important scholars in the various fields of ethics, we have nurtured an interest in the study of the ethics of Judaism on the part of graduate students in History of Religions: Judaism. Many of these students come to us with knowledge of halakhic *and* musar *literature, with answers to ethical issues. With our colleagues, they learn to ask appropriate questions in the study of that literature. A second area of strength is in the history of theology, and this has produced emphasis upon the study of nineteenth and twentieth century Judaic thought in the context of the Protestant and Catholic religious thought of the same period. A third area under intellectual development is in Hellenistic Judaism and Early Christianity, in which our resources are exceptional. Finally, we realized that while students in Judaism were well prepared in the limited exegesis of biblical texts, their knowledge of the modern, critical study of the history of Israelite religion and literature was severely limited. Since work on dissertations in Talmudic religion carries forward established critical methods of biblical research, we have begun to emphasize greater mastery of those methods in their own context. These are some of the ways in which the foregoing programmatic statement has to be revised.*

And there is yet one more. When I came to Brown, I did not imagine that my colleagues would develop serious research-interests in the study of Judaism. I found that as I was able to participate in the intellectual life of our group, I was able to contribute to the education, in the study of Judaism, of colleagues whose primary interests lay in the study of Christianity, just as my own education in the study of important problems in the history of Christianity was improved. The result has been for colleagues to include the study of Judaism in courses not primarily devoted to Judaism at all, for example, in the study of the modernization of Christian thought, Jewish and Judaic thought comes under consideration; in the study of comparative religious ethics, the ethics of Judaism is included. Further, courses primarily devoted to aspects of the study of Judaism now are given by specialists in other areas, who, having done their homework, contribute sophisticated method to the analysis of Judaic religious texts and problems. With a certain pride I note that the curriculum in the study of Judaism at Brown is not wholly in the hands of Jewish teachers of Judaism to Jewish students; Christian and gentile scholars give the larger number of courses in History of Religions: Judaism. (An appropriate development—which I do not foresee— will be the contrary phenomenon.) The integration of the study of Judaism into courses not defined around the study of Judaism and the active contribution of scholars of other subjects and disciplines to instruction in Judaism seem to me a considerable testimony to the promise of the academic setting for Judaic learning: vedayya sarah beshaᶜatah.

VIII

AUTODIDACTS IN GRADUATE SCHOOL

One grave problem confronting graduate education in all aspects of Jewish studies is the persistence of an anti-professional pattern. That pattern consists of the following educational stages: first, elementary and sometimes secondary schooling in Jewish schools, including yeshivot; second, a baccalaureate degree in a discipline not associated with Jewish studies and normally in an aspect of that discipline not applied or connected to Jewish data; and third, a graduate degree made up of courses following the same or a similar baccalaureate pattern, under the supervision of a scholar in no way related to Jewish studies. The sole connection to Jewish studies will be a dissertation on a Jewish topic. Consequently, the dissertation is based upon elementary-school studies of Judaica and such other learning as may be gained outside of the curriculum. It is guided by a scholar not informed about the state of knowledge in its field. The author turns out never to have taken even a single graduate seminar in Judaic studies. He therefore emerges as an autodidact, without benefit of instruction at the graduate level, frequently at the college level, in the state of scholarship in his (or any other) area of Jewish studies. He then goes forth to teach a subject in which he has not even tried to achieve professional qualifications. So he does not perceive his own amateurism.

Examples of this pattern are numerous: one is a dissertation on a Hassidic rabbi in the department of comparative literature at Princeton University; another is a dissertation on a sixteenth-century rabbi to be prepared under the supervision of a distinguished scholar of the reformation at the University of Chicago. Here the theory is that

145

the rabbi in question was a contemporary of Martin Luther. Anyone who knows a great deal about Luther is apt to know something pertinent to the life of that rabbi, who, to be sure, lived many hundreds of miles away and in an utterly different world.

A correlated pattern, which I regard as only somewhat less unprofessional, involves graduate education in Jewish studies, for instance, in Jewish history, followed by a dissertation in which the dissertation supervisor performs the task of certification, but not of instruction. That is, the supervisor himself knows little about the topic. He does not exhibit mastery of the sources pertinent to that topic. He frequently does not know even the languages of those sources.

What I object to in what has here been characterized as an unprofessional pattern of education is this: According to such a pattern, Jewish studies, in their several aspects and modes of investigation, not only do not demand the same level of professional preparation required in other humanities, but also do not require more than an autodidact's level of competence. The fields of Jewish learning have no scholarly traditions, no disciplines. They are not marked by significant steps forward, so that every beginner may claim to stand at the very beginning of the scholarly task. That pattern furthermore implies the doctoral degree stands merely for professional certification ("a union card"), rather than for the completion of an important stage in education. Any mode of education is as good as any other, so long as the Ph.D. finally is awarded. The holder then is indeed as well qualified in one field of Jewish learning as in any other. The qualifications have, after all, been attained through his efforts alone, without initiation into the traditions of learning, without criticism by informed critics who themselves have faced and tried to solve the same problems.

I maintain that graduate education in Jewish studies should follow the established norms of other humanities. Graduate seminars in Jewish studies should prepare the students for scholarly undertakings in those studies. The dissertation should be subject to the supervision of instructors familiar with the scholarly literature, the sources, and, especially the conceptual and methodological problems inherent in the sources, pertinent to the topic of the dissertation. The doctoral degree is not solely a mode of certification. It marks the attainment of a stage in the student's learning and indicates successful achievement in his scholarship. He should now be prepared to carry forward the tasks of his field, not all by himself but in collaboration with learned men and women, living or dead, who confront or have contributed to, the accomplishment of those tasks. Jewish studies in the modern modes are not primitive. Much has been accomplished. Nothing today justifies the autodidactic modes of study probably necessary a century ago for the founders of the Jewish sciences.

Now I admit insistence upon graduate studies with established scholars in established fields is going to limit the range of topics open to the beginning scholar. Our numbers are not great; we all specialize in modest areas of learning. Important aspects of Jewish studies simply are not represented in American and Canadian universities and seminaries. In some measure historical accidents alone will account for the availability of specialization in some areas, not in others. Yet in all there is a certain appropriateness in the fields we do stress in our several graduate programs. For all of them may be investigated within the resources of our universities and by people whose education is in the main in American and Canadian primary and secondary schools and colleges.

The qualified scholar knows full well that in time he may modify the direction of his studies. Upon the basis of sound education in methods of investigation and modes of critical thinking, he certainly may turn not only to new topics within his antecedent area of interest, but to entirely new areas of interest, requiring the mastery of new languages, new histories, new fields of literary scholarship. It is entirely commonplace to do so. What is uncommon, except in our field, is the assumption of graduate students that graduate instruction is something to be endured, not enjoyed; that the less your professors know about your own area of scholarly interest, the better off you are.

Finally, it should be pointed out that, faced with the choice of programs in Jewish studies or in some other area, at least some doctoral candidates prefer to study in a program outside of Judaica, while fully intending to present themselves as qualified professors of

Jewish studies. For instance, the dissertation on the sixteenth-century rabbi at Chicago, to be offered to professors without the qualifications to read and criticize it, should be presented, after appropriate graduate seminars, to available specialists who have those qualifications, for example at Harvard. Many topics not done by Americans and Canadians are investigated in the State of Israel, Britain or France.

The student to which I refer seems to me an extension of the old Talmudic *ilui,* the child so brilliant that no one can teach him. Many stories, some of them true, record how from the age of ten or eleven, a great scholar never again learned with a rabbi, for no one could teach him anything. I have no doubt that such prodigies of learning, such stunning precocity, did sometimes characterize Talmudic circles. But they are sufficiently rare in the humanities to call into question the pretention of the aspiring *ilui* who comes to graduate school planning at the least to teach the teacher, and at best thoroughly to intimidate him. This obviously is easiest to accomplish with respectful professors not in Jewish studies at all, therefore not informed to begin with that an *alef* is different from an *ayin.* But the scholar in Judaica sometimes offers himself for this purpose, for he may much more want graduate students than he wants to teach them anything. Nor should we ignore the disrespectful professor not in Jewish studies who takes for granted one may pick up Jewish learning on the side, while mastering the important data and methods of some more important field—his own. I know exactly this prescription is applied at Michigan in Classics or Ancient History, although there are doubtless many other examples.

My contribution to the discussion of the nature and structure of Jewish studies in the graduate school therefore consists in pointing out this simple fact: Not all graduate students intending to offer themselves as Jewish scholars actually undertake graduate work in Jewish studies at all. An apparently significant group at reputable universities does not. So one task before us is to persuade colleagues and students alike that the study of the Jews and of Judaism is not only a hobby, but also a profession. It requires not merely insight and brilliance, but also disciplined preparation, accurate learning, mastery of the available scholarly traditions, and, above all, criticism from people who, in reasonable measure, have these three things.

COMMENT

This brief paper, unfortunately, requires no correction. Matters have not changed. The fault, however, in no way lies with the scholars of the various areas of Jewish studies, all the more so with graduate programs in those areas. At fault are those who treat the field with condescension, asking less of the study of Judaism than they do of the study of other problems in the field of religion (or in other fields). Hopefully, good scholarship and teaching will drive out the bad. The example of well-prepared young men and women, who have attained significant and professional competence in the study of Judaism, may go far to bring into disrepute amateurs, autodidacts, and those who find themselves so brilliant as in advance to dismiss all their teachers. I tend to think that it is the inexperience of colleagues in dealing with a subject still in its infancy in the university that accounts for toleration of what elsewhere would be dismissed as charlatanism. If matters have not changed, there is yet time. There always is time.

Part Five

PERSONAL CONCLUSIONS

PERSONAL CONCLUSIONS

Introduction

Throughout the foregoing papers, I have argued that objectivity is ambiguous and, if no more is required for objectivity than restraint from proselytizing, simply trivial. I do not claim to be objective about anything. I know facts; I believe in certain propositions; I stand for quite concrete and specific values; and I do so without apology. I do not admire those who claim to take up no particular position and to stand for nothing, both because I do not believe that claim, and because I do not honor self-professed nihilism. What is it that I do believe? It is contained in the final two papers.

The first is a kind of apologia for myself and my life. It is not a statement of desperation or exasperation, but of confidence and hope. To be sure, it is occasional and ephemeral, not likely to be interesting long into the future. I justify including it solely as an effort to exemplify that faith which I do profess and for which I do give my life. The second is equally ephemeral, equally personal. It is merely a little chat with an entering class of Brown University. All which I have said about universities and about the place of the study of Judaism in them is contained in this paper. Readers familiar with the passages of biblical and especially Talmudic literature paraphrased or even directly quoted in this paper will understand the sort of advocacy and commitment hinted at in the earlier papers.

The issues of the academic study of Judaism are not at all academic. They are, in different language, perennial and enduring. How can we ask ourselves not to care about those issues, not to take a stance about them, or ask others to believe that Jewish scholars of Jewish subjects really do not care about the Jews? Yet we also are university people, men and women, who stand with our colleagues and who profess to take seriously the things which, at its best, the university in the West has represented: reverence for reason, respect for contrary opinion, criticism, above all self-criticism, all in the quest for learning and for meaning. If the chronic dilemmas of the Jewish situation have appeared in these papers, as I believe they have, then those of us privileged to live out our lives in universities have to analyze and discuss those issues in a way consonant with the setting in which we do our work. We must do so in a manner loyal to the values of those many men and women, of the past but especially among our colleagues, to whom we look for guidance, example, and intelligent counsel.

These two papers are meant to do the opposite of what they seem. The former is an address in a synagogue. It is a message of the faith of a university teacher. It could have been said by anyone. The latter is an address in the most unlikely setting for a sermon by a "rabbi" (of a curious sort) out of the sources of Judaism. It could have been said only by a Jew. If those who heard these papers understood them in accord with their setting, in a synagogue, in a lecture hall, and not as ironic gestures, quietly defiant of the context, that is a fair measure of success.

I have omitted the customary critical afterword in these papers. They are too intensely personal for me to criticize them. I am sure, alas, critics, in public or in private, will not be lacking. So be it: we are what we are.

IX

CREATIVITY IN THE CONTEXT OF JUDAISM

[Address at Anshe Emet Synagogue, Chicago, Illinois, October 27, 1974, on the occasion of receiving the Solomon Goldman Award for Jewish Creativity.]

Since we have just passed the end of the thirty days of mourning for one of the truly great creative minds of modern Jewry, Harry Wolfson, let me begin with two things he said to me. When I was young and still hoped for understanding of what I was trying to accomplish, I complained to him at the nearly uniform rejection of everything I tried to do. His reply was this: "If you want to be accepted and even liked, then do not say anything which has not already been said, nor do anything which has not already been done. Do not disagree with anyone. Do not say anything new. Best of all, do nothing at all. Then you will be a great scholar in the eyes of the world. On the other hand, if you want to be a great scholar, do things your own way, and wait. People will get used to you." He said that to me about ten years ago. In the months before he died, I visited him from time to time. Since he had seen virtually nothing of my work, I gave him *From Politics to Piety: The Emergence of Pharisaic Judaism*. Despite his physical infirmities, he struggled through the book. I believe it was one of the last books he ever read. When I saw him a week later, he said two things to me, both very brief. First, "This book should have been written seventy-five years ago." Second, "My best advice to you is this: do exactly what you want, the way you want, in precisely the form you want, and do not pay attention to anyone." These were the words of a dying man, and I

155

believe them. Neither he nor I spoke again of merely waiting; we both knew there was, and would be, nothing to wait for.

That is all I wish to say about myself. Let me now speak of "creativity," first of all by rejecting the word. It is pretentious, all too general and generalized. I prefer to use simpler and more concrete words. Let us talk of making things, doing things, finding out how things work, explaining things, the seeking of understanding and of insight. For within Judaism there is only one creation, and it is God's. My dictionary tells me that creation is "the act of creating, the act of bringing the world into existence from nothing." Only God is the creator. Humankind makes things out of what God made from nothing. We imitate God but cannot be more than *like* God. I remind you of Rashi's explanation of the verse, "Lest they become like God." Here he adds, "creators of worlds." In the context of Judaism, we require a more humble definition of "creativity" or "creation," and my dictionary gives fair help: "the act of making, inventing, or producing." That is less awesome language, claiming in our behalf something appropriate to us all: making things, inventing things, producing things. This each man and woman does. But some do what already has been done, do it in the old, safe, established way. And some do not. Curiously, this world belongs to those who do little, add nothing, and prove amiable to all. I do not know what world belongs to the others.

That is not to suggest that making things is only making new things. For Judaism, making things is never making totally new things. We stand in a tradition, and that fact by itself imposes severe limits upon innovation. Yet Judaism is an ever-renewed tradition, so, by definition, each generation does much that is new. Let me draw upon two works which I find dazzling not only in their erudition, in their mastery of the old, but also in their renovation and innovation, to explain how within Judaism people do make things, invent things, produce things. The one is Maimonides' *Mishnah Torah,* the other is Lieberman's *Tosefet Rishonim.* Neither work was what one might call a success in its own time. *Mishnah Torah* was burned. *Tosefet Rishonim* should have won for its author the most prestigious professorship in Jewish learning, but it did not,

and it is a work remarkably neglected, though, to be sure, cere-
moniously and copiously praised by people who have never opened
it. Its genius is, I think, yet to be fully appreciated. What do these
works have in common? What do they teach us about the way,
within Judaism, we make, invent, produce?

Let us, first, consider the simplest aspect, the matter of the author's
form and intent. *Mishnah Torah* proposes to take the place of Mishnah, to reduce to easily accessible codes the whole of the law, so to
make room, within the Jewish intellect, for other concerns entirely.
It is an arrogant and destructive work. The form, moreover, not only
is logical, but, as everyone knows, exceptionally simple and lucid.
Tosefet Rishonim pretends to accomplish an old and standard task,
to assemble various versions or readings of passages of Tosefta. Its
superficial claim is the sort of humble erudition which threatens no
one and challenges nothing. If *Mishnah Torah* adopts a remarkably
new form and language, *Tosefet Rishonim* does the opposite.

Let us turn, second, to the matter of substance. What is old, and
what is new, in the two great works before us? *Mishnah Torah* is
not much more than a set of citations, restatements, and revisions of
passages in classical Talmudic literature, particularly Mishnah-
Tosefta and related compilations. If we systematically went through
Mishnah Torah and set in bold-face type everything which is either
a direct citation or a paraphrase of the inherited legal literature,
nearly the whole book would be in bold-face type. Yet anyone who
has worked through major segments of Mishnah-Tosefta and *Mishnah Torah* knows the opposite. By his arrangement, restatement,
subtle reorganization, of existing materials, Maimonides succeeded
in redirecting the entire course of the interpretation of all that had
gone before. He simply re-founded the interpretative process—both
form and substance—of Mishnah-Tosefta—that is, of Jewish law.
And he implanted upon the interpretation of the legal literature the
stunningly fit logic, clarity, and order of his own remarkable mind.
To study the law with Maimonides is to make friends with one of
the most beautiful minds in human history. My dear colleague,
Professor Otto Neugebauer, who works in areas remote from Judaism but who has, for his own reasons, studied passages in Mai-

monides, once met me on the street and asked, What are you doing? I replied, I am spending most of my time with Rambam (Maimonides). His immediate, sparkling reply was, "Oh, he's a wonderful fellow, isn't he?" To both of us, he indeed *is,* for he never died, and we do not perceive him in the past tense. To summarize, what is "creative" in the sense of innovative in *Mishnah Torah* is expressed, effected primarily through the daring and imaginative confrontation with the given. Nothing is new, but everything is renewed. Nothing is innovative, yet everything is refreshed, given a new life.

We come back to *Tosefet Rishonim,* printed in the old way, in its harsh paper and blotchy ink, expressed in the old way, primarily through sets of arcane allusions or references to other documents (in the manner of other great commentators, for instance, 'Aqiva Egger), seemingly nothing more than a telephone book. But enter into a passage of Tosefta, try to understand what it is saying, by itself and in relationship to the Mishnah to which it is a supplement, and you will discover something truly surprising. *Tosefet Rishonim* turns out to be an amazingly subtle rethinking of every problem worth rethinking, a reworking in a few brief words of the entire exegetical tradition (such as it is) of Tosefta, and in innumerable passages, the provision of the first intelligent explanation. What Maimonides did in his way, namely, to revise and renew the study of the major documents of the *halakhah,* Lieberman did, systematically and reverently, in his. He took over every bit and piece of inherited materials—both texts and comments and explanations— and reworked it all. Its unpretention therefore is deceiving. Like *Mishnah Torah,* it is an arrogant and destructive work, for it renders obsolete and uninteresting most of the antecedent explanation of Tosefta. Like *Mishnah Torah* it lays out the main lines of the study and interpretation of Tosefta, I believe, for all time. Like *Mishnah Torah,* it is a *ma'ayan hamitgaber,* an ever-flowing well; every page is full of new insight, even new method. When one might expect that, after so much that has gone before, Lieberman will run out of new ideas and simply repeat his established methods and procedures on new materials, we find the exact opposite, an ever-flowing stream not only of new insights, but even of new methods. And, I have to add, planted on each page is a small 'time-bomb' of humor, for the author's mind, if not his style, is a well-spring of grace and charm.

I regret that it would be futile to lay before you examples or evidence for the propositions just now stated about Maimonides and Lieberman. Their work is at the heights of the law, and we should have to ascend through much labor to reach the level of discourse, to grasp and understand not only their solutions, but even—and especially—the questions they propose to solve. What we can learn from these two examples of creativity, of making things, within Judaism is clear. The person, man or woman, who proposes to make, produce, or invent things within Judaism must come with four qualities: arrogance and humility, radical and conservative traits of heart and mind.

He or she must be so arrogant, even so destructive, as to see flaws in the given, in what everyone believes is adequate and right. The makers and the doers must take a stance apart from the world and even against the world of established truths and accepted ways of seeing things. There is no other way. For if all is perfect, there is nothing more to be done. If everyone is right, then what can be so wrong as to require repair? It is only the person of extreme arrogance, self-confidence, certainty or his or her own vocation, who can so act as to inform the world of its own imperfections, therefore of its perfectability. The old order must change, change always. The only lasting perfection is in death; then there is no change. Yet the makers and the doers must be able to listen and to learn. They have to understand that if the world is imperfect, they are part of the world. Nothing is so sterile as the person who finds satisfaction in what already has been accomplished. And sterile indeed is the person even remotely satisfied with his own work. We are our own most severe critics, and testimony to our criticism is our continuing to make things. If what we have done is beyond criticism, is, within our aspirations, perfect, then why do anything more? Yet the people who make things make many things, and the people who make things which will last are those who make each thing new and better than what already is finished. Behind us is the old and flawed, above all, that old and imperfect thing we ourselves have done. Before us is the hope to do better. Arrogance and humility are opposite sides of the same coin.

So too are the radical and the conservative traits of heart and mind. Radical means to go to the root. Anyone who wants to make something worthwhile had best learn how to find the fundamental problem, the most basic and irreducible minimum. The greatest achievements are also the simplest, the most elementary. People who propose to begin had best begin afresh, from the beginning. Conservative means to preserve what is good in what already has been done. To be conservative is not to be one who stands still, but to prefer to work within the givens, to see oneself not as creating out of nothing whatsoever, which only God can do, but to be *like* God in making things at all.

Thus far I have spoken about "creativity" within Judaism. Matters therefore are abstract, seem uncontroversial, amiable, and unexceptional. Let us turn to the here-and-now, the social context in which people make, invent, and produce things primarily for Jews, that is, the context of Judaism. For if we do not take seriously the fact that people do not make things except where they are, for the world in which they are, we shall not understand the resentment expressed by people who have made things and who now make things, the powerful sense of discouragement, alienation, rejection, and loneliness contained in those few words with which I began, which Harry Wolfson said to me at brink of the grave: Do what you want, the way you want, when you want, and do not pay attention to what anyone says.

There are two sides to the matter of the context and reception of the work of the people who do work. Built in to the person who makes things is a deep sense of discontent. It is part of his being, makes possible his or her capacity to make, produce, invent, generates his or her curiosity about how things work and desire to take things apart and put them back together. However benign and welcoming society—Jewish society—might be (and it is not benign at all), the doers and the workers could not appreciate the reception. Endemic to and·inseparable from the aspiration to make things is the criticism of what has already been made, by others and by oneself, as I said. That aspiration carries its negative charge in alienation and resentment. I do not see how things can be otherwise, under the very best circumstances (which are unimaginable). Whether or not God, in making something out of nothing, perceived within the Godhead an imperfection is something for the Qabbalah to explain to us; but those who seek, within the limits of mortality, to be like God most certainly create because of the imperfections of creation. And the reason, I think, the priestly narrator tells us that God looked upon all that he had made and said that it was good, very good, is probably the astonishment therein to be discerned. For God is surely the first and last creator ever and finally to call what he had made good, very good. And, we all know, even God continues the works of creation at sunrise and sunset and in the course of nature. There may be limits to divine discontent, no more floods, for instance, but there is none to that of mortal man and woman.

Accordingly, the people within Jewry who make, invent and produce place an unacceptable demand upon Jewish society. They require those who are satisfied to share their dissatisfaction, those who are at home and comfortable to accept the product of alienation and resentment. In the simplest language, those who are, explicitly or implicitly, subject to the criticism constituted by the new are supposed to love the critic. Not only is that demand unacceptable, it also is an incomprehensible and unearned tribute. For those who make, produce, and invent genuinely believe there is someone to accept, consume, and make use of what is made. The resentment expresses deep engagement. The alienation is a statement of commitment and involvement. The critic comes with a terrible, ferocious love. The disappointment in the life of the maker, doer, and inventor is the highest tribute he or she can pay.

Yet it is so that the way to be loved is to affirm what is, to be accepted, one must accept, to get along, we must go along. And none of these is possible, by definition, for the maker and doer. Requited love is stifling. But the engagement, commitment, and involvement of love generate not only strife but life. I think, in this connection, of Maurice Samuel, surely one of the truly elegant and graceful, brilliant and creative people of our day. I asked his widow,

Edith Samuel, whether Maurice Samuel might have left us a larger literary legacy had he been able to make his living other than on the lecture platform. She told me, No, Maurice loved to lecture. He loved to go out among the people and speak with them. It was the Jewish people which was the source of his grace, elegance, capacity to make beautiful and profound things. In this same context, I refer to the discussion, in the mid-1950s, of making the Jewish Theological Seminary financially independent, through endowments. (How lovely it is to remember there were times in which such things could be contemplated!) My teacher and friend Moshe Davis strongly opposed the effort. The Seminary, he said, must always depend, from year to year, upon the people of the Conservative movement, so that the Seminary would never lose touch with the realities of its people, would always derive its spiritual lifeblood, as much as its money, from the people. The moment in which the Seminary (or any other Jewish institution) cut itself off from the community would be the hour of its death. So it is for individuals and for the institutions in which people learn how to make, do, invent, produce. The ultimate source of the power to make things is engagement, yielding tension and strife, with the people.

In this regard the Israelis have a fair criticism of American Jewish cultural life (such as it is). They find it disembodied, remote from reality, because there is no national, cultural, and social integration. The *Golah* makes things at the margins of society. In the State of Israel, the creative person is at the very center of life. Our apologists make a virtue of alienation. At the center of things is blandness. Only the marginal person perceives the potential, the new. The one in the middle, so far as he can see, sees only what is old, the same as everyone else. I find myself torn between the two views. But the Israelis have much to tell us, I think, about what it is to make, invent, and produce in a normal setting, and their reservations about our self-serving arguments in behalf of marginality and alienation are not without good reason.

Yet surely there must be limits, and these limits must be found, to the permissible distance between the people who make and do, on the one side, and between the Jewish community, on the other. Thus far I have stressed the responsibility of the makers and the doers to preserve their roots among those for whom they make things. It would be disingenuous for me to imply that is where I think the really painful issue is located. For the really great gifts which are given to us have come from people who never got, or even hoped to get, their just reward, in understanding and appreciation of their work, in recognition for the right reasons, in respect.

Those to whom we do pay respect do not always seem to deserve it; yet they do deserve what they get, for it is not really respect but adulation, not critical appreciation but stifling praise. Those who make it the easy way—by repeating what has been done and calling it new, by appealing to the familiar and the acceptable in the pretense of saying something fresh, by meretricious wisdom and sentimentalism and bathos—they get their just reward. They end up repeating themselves, filling up pages with words, not writing, babbling and blathering their way, along with all fads, into obscurity and well-earned oblivion.

Time must test all things, all hopes. Consider what was said, in their own day, about the most influential and important ideas—and the people who made them up—of the last century. Gunkel never had a decent position. Who remembers his critics? Who reads the books they praised, while damning his? Charles Ives (to take a New England example, so near my heart) never, until the end of his life, even heard a line of his music properly performed in a concert hall. Much of his music was unknown for fifty or sixty years. We know that every major development in composition of our own times, even of our own decade, turns out to have been in his mind. He was, to be sure, a deadly critic of the music of his own day and of most of what went before. He walked very much by himself. After a certain point, he simply ceased to make up music at all. Today New England and the world live from his music; our New England radio stations play his compositions nearly as often as Mozart's or Bach's. He transforms our ears, our perceptions of music. In the New England heritage are many Charles Ives's; on the capitol of Rhode Island is a statue, called The Independent Man; on the license plates of New Hampshire is printed, Live free or die. Sometimes I wish all the

Jewish people could have a little of the granite of New England in their minds, could be as hardheaded as our Yankee neighbors of Vermont and Rhode Island.

But they do not, and that is a painful problem. For why is it that we damn the Philip Roth's or the Herbert Gold's, who see us so deeply and so truly, if with an astringent and searing vision? Why does the purity of their perception so offend us? Why do we not muster the maturity to withhold praise—if only by a healthy instinct—from those who please us too much and who seem to know how to do it? And it is not only so in fiction. When we think of Jewish music (with all the problems attendant upon defining what we mean by "Jewish music"), why is it that we who fill the concert halls of America accept in the synagogues and Temples the liturgical equivalent of *Fiddler on a Roof*? Why have we taken over as expressive of our musical aspirations the most godawful banalities of Israeli *kitsch*-culture? And then there is philosophy, scholarship, the world of ideas. Let us spare the culture-heroes the indignity of mentioning their names. Those without style get their just reward, as I said, by being praised for style, and those without ideas are praised for their profound ideas. There is an inexorable justice in this, and perhaps it is God's wish that the reverse should also be the case. For it surely is the case. The most learned and truly Jewish philosopher of our time was Abraham Joshua Heschel. Read the early reviews of his greatest works, by people well known today, and ask yourselves whether the reviewers cared even to try to listen to him, to hear what he was saying. For as I reread them in preparing this address, what I found was a complaint that Heschel did not choose to address himself to the issues the critics thought he should treat. Historians have given us beautiful works of historical literature—I think of Howard Sachar's histories of the Middle East—and we have not read them. Historians have given us ideology, reasons for praising ourselves and indulging our need to feel superior to other people, and we have read them. Theologians have given us works of logic and meticulous thought, and we have not heard or read them. I think of Arthur A. Cohen and Frederick Plotkin. Theologians have given us fake arguments about why we should be Jewish, and we have flocked to their lectures. Writers and poets are among us who have told us the truth, and we have not listened to them. Writers and poets are among us who give us doggerel and journalism (may my forefathers forgive me for using the word in its worst sense, to mean something light, transient, and inconsequential), and we have bought their books and cried over their doggerel or recited it in our "creative worship services." A. M. Klein and Jacob Glatstein, to name two whom we never deserved, might as well be on the moon, so far as we have been concerned. Yet the best of our prayer books have taken over their work, and in those prayer books their words burn with fire.

What then? Shall we condemn ourselves to what we deserve, want, and pay for? Or shall we ask whether we can give to the makers and producers and inventors of what is honest and authentic, if cantankerous, difficult, unfamiliar, flawed and human, what they demand without compromise? That is not adulation but fair criticism, not mindless acceptance but thoughtful response. We should. I do not know whether we shall.

I know only this: despite uncomprehension and disinterest, despite those who express envy through denigration and those who express admiration through jealousy and through vilification, despite the many who can respect themselves only by tearing down the works of others, despite the world which sees the one who does new things as crazy, despite betrayal and disappointment and disbelief— despite it all, and in the face of it all, and against it all, the work will go forward. Because in doing this thing, in making or inventing or producing what ears have not heard and eyes have not read and mind never before has understood or even thought of, the makers and doers and inventors are doing what they were made to do, to be like God in the peculiar image in which he made them. There is no choice but to be what one is, to do what one must do: exactly what you want, the way you want, in the form you want, and do not pay attention to anyone. That means, to be sure, not to pay attention even to awards for Jewish creativity, but I thank you nonetheless.

X

TO THE CLASS OF 1976

This week marks the commencement of your four years at Brown University. My purpose is to introduce those four years.

You come to take your places in an on-going enterprise, a university. It was here before you came. It probably will be here after you leave. But you can and will make your mark upon it. You can enhance its life, or blight its future. Each generation of faculty, students, and administration has that power. For universities are fragile. They rise and fall, go through times of excellence and mediocrity. This you already know, for you applied to many universities and colleges, and chose the best for you, so you realize that significant differences separate one university from the next. We have no "Truth in Merchandising Law" to cover universities; they all call themselves by the same name. But the differences are there, and in the next four years, you are one of the givens, one of the data, that will characterize and distinguish Brown.

But your first impression must be otherwise. As you come to Brown, you must perceive yourselves to be the last and least in a long procession of men and women. You see buildings you did not build, a great library, carefully nurtured for two hundred years, which you did not create, a faculty you did not assemble, a community you did not form. Everything seems so well established, so permanent. But that impression is illusory. Just a few years ago students in other universities burned and ravaged the buildings built for their use, closed the libraries, shut down the class-rooms. So it is clear that students have the power to destroy. By their excellence they also have the power to build. Faculties come to teach the best

166

students they can find; high salaries and pleasant working conditions alone do not suffice to keep talented men and women in universities composed of bored and sullen students. If you are purposeful, if you are mindful, if you show yourselves to be critical, thoughtful, interested students, you will give the university the good name of a place where important things take place, where the life of the mind is fully and richly lived. And within my experience, Brown's richest asset is its students. I cannot exaggerate the intellectual excellence and the personal charm of the students I have known here, and I do not speak for myself alone. So do not see yourselves as unimportant. Your coming is very important; it is the decisive event of the present time. What other generations have created, the wealth they lavished on this place, the care and concern they gave it, the endowment of centuries—these opportunities now fall into your hands. Do not waste what other men and women have made. Do not take for granted the unearned increment of the ages. For four years you live on the labor of other, earlier generations, who gave to the future what, for their part, they had gotten from the past.

What happens in Brown University? First, let me say what does not happen. The problems of the world are not going to be solved by you. You are not going here to make a better world, to improve the condition of 'man,' or to solve the problem of poverty. Indeed, the money society (not to mention your parents) spends on you here is diverted from other worthwhile projects. The endowment of this university could purchase better housing for the poor or raise the welfare benefits for the needy; it could go for many worthwhile social purposes. But it is set aside so that you, mature men and women perfectly capable of working at some useful and remunerative task, may remain idle. You are kept unemployed, others have to pay for your keep, so that you may read books, work in labs, listen and talk, write and think. A university is an expression of a highly aristocratic, anti-egalitarian ideal; it stands for the opposite of the equality of all men and women, rather, their inequalities in matters of the mind and spirit. A great many people past and present have set aside their wealth and their energies for that aristocratic ideal, that excellent minds have the opportunity for growth and improvement, that the intellect be cultivated. Your years at Brown could likewise go to socially more relevant purposes. You could, after all, take a job and earn a living for yourselves. But you sacrifice that income. Your four years of idleness represent a joint decision, made both by you and by your family and by 'society,' that it is better for now to think, so later on you may do; it is wiser now to hold back, so later on you may go much further onward.

Yet this thing which will not happen here at Brown—your immediate engagement with the great tasks of society—imposes on you an extraordinary struggle: the struggle to postpone easy accomplishment and quick distinction. True achievement depends on depth of learning, on capacity for clear thinking, on ability to pursue knowledge where curiosity leads, above all in implacable criticism of all givens. True achievement depends on these things, rather than on the premature acceptance of public responsibility. Young men and women want to go forth, to do great things. We keep you here to study, to think about things. You come full of energy. You would find it natural to take on great tasks. You want nothing less than to sit long hours in the discipline of the mind. To read and write, to argue and expound, to confront the various claims to truth in a sophisticated, critical spirit—these represent stern tests for men and women at your age (or any other). You are called to an unnatural repression of your selves, to overcome the natural instincts of your age.

Nothing is so hard as to see your contemporaries at their life's work and to postpone your own. And remember, you represent only a small proportion of your age-group. The majority will not be with you this fall; many are at work, or at considerably less demanding universities than this one. Nothing is so inviting as to pick up the burdens of the world and enter the workaday life, nor so demanding of self-discipline as to deny them. You come to learn, not with the curious but empty minds of pre-teens, but with the strength of maturing, able men and women. But the conquest of the self, by overcoming ambition, distraction, and sheer laziness, and by winning your best ability to the service of the mind—this great struggle will prove most satisfying for those of you who win it. Later on no enemy will prove so difficult as the enemy within. No challenge will prove harder to overcome than the one you now fight within yourself. In the university you have now to vanquish the undisciplined impulse to ready yourself for struggle with, for service to, the world.

Above all, if you succeed in acquiring the critical mode of thought which is our ware, you will have the one thing you will need to become important people: the capacity to stand firm in what you think right, in what you propose to accomplish in life. Today you have to postpone the quest for worldly success. Later on it may not come; you may have to walk quite by yourself. When the world is against you, you will have to rely for strength only upon your own convictions. I speak from experience: the world is not going to give you many satisfactions, especially if you propose to change it. For if you do, you thereby claim things are not yet perfect. What everybody thinks is true really is not so. What everybody wants to do, thinks it right and best to do, is not the best way at all. Great men and women achieve that greatness above the mob, not within it. And they cannot be loved on that account. The world will love its own, those who tell and do the things reassuring to the mediocre. Here you begin to struggle with the given, with the natural, with how you feel and how your friends feel. Do not expect the success that comes from easy accomplishment and ready recognition. What will justify the effort, if all there is before you is defeat and renewed struggle? You must not learn to expect success in order to justify your efforts. You must learn to need only to think the effort necessary, whatever the outcome. Great things are not accomplished by the shouters but by the workers. But to learn to work—that is a hard task indeed.

I have said what will not happen in Brown University. What then does happen here? Only one thing that makes worthwhile the years and money you devote to your university education: you should learn to ask questions and to find the answers to them. Everything else is frivolous, peripheral, for the shouters and the headline-chasers. And a great many of the questions you will ask and learn to answer are irrelevant to shouting and to headlines.

Now what are these questions? They are not the generalities, but the specificities, not the abstractions but the concrete and detailed matters that delimit the frontiers of knowledge. Do not ask, what is man, or what is truth, what is history, or what is biology? Your teachers may give you answers to these great questions, but these are rote and routine. And your teachers cannot tell you what good is the answer. What we want is only to *know*: not necessarily how to harness atomic energy, but about energy and matter, not necessarily how to "cure cancer," but about the nature of living matter.

Notice I did not say we seek "the truth" or "the truth about energy," but only "about . . . ." I mean to emphasize the tentativeness, the modesty, the austerity of our work. I begin, after all, as a critic of my own perceptions, only then do I criticize those of others. In what I do I seek to know the limits of knowledge, to define just what is factual about the facts purportedly in my hands. For the asking of questions, the seeking of answers, begins in a very deep skepticism. If I thought we knew all we need to know, what should I find to ask? The asking of questions is a subversive activity. It subverts accepted truths, the status quo.

Your teachers at Brown do not propose to tell you what is generally agreed upon as 'the truth' about this or that. In this regard you must not assume they are like your teachers in high school or prep school, whose job it was to communicate established knowledge, to teach you what is already agreed upon. Your teachers in Brown are different because they are actively engaged in the disciplined study and questioning of the given. They are trying to find out new things, trying to reassess the truth of the old. The high school teacher you already know tends to take for granted the correctness of what he tells you. The teacher at Brown is probably going to ask whether what he tells you is so, how he claims to know it, above all, *how he himself has found it out*. He is an active participant in learning, not a passive recipient and transmitter of other peoples' facts. How he thinks, how he analyzes a problem, therefore is what you have to learn from him. It is all he had to teach you. *What* he thinks you probably can find out in books, his or someone else's. *Why* he thinks so—this alone he can tell you. Before now, the result of learning was central. Here the modes and procedures of thinking are at issue.

I said what makes your years here important is the asking of questions and the finding of answers. But there is a second important process, flowing from the first, in which you have got to learn to participate: the process of communication. It is not enough to have found ways of thought. One has to express them as well. As the great Yale historian Edmund S. Morgan says, "Scholarship begins in curiosity, but it ends in communication." You do not need to justify asking questions. But if you think you have found answers, you have not got the right to remain silent. I do not guarantee people will listen to you. The greater likelihood is that they will ignore what they do not understand or vilify what they do not like. But you are not free from the task of saying what you think. This will take two forms, and you must master both: writing and speaking. You have got to learn to express your ideas in a clear and vigorous way. You have got to do this both in writing and in the class-room (and outside as well). I promise you, your teachers at Brown will give you many opportunities to exercise and improve your skills at both.

On the importance of communicating ideas as the center of the educational experience, let me again quote Edmund Morgan:

> Communication is not merely the desire and responsibility of the scholar; it is his discipline . . . Without communication his pursuit of truth withers into eccentricity. He necessarily spends much of his time alone . . . But he needs to be rubbing constantly against other minds . . . He needs to be made to explain himself . . . The scholar . . . needs company to keep him making sense . . . people to challenge him at every step, who will take nothing for granted.

Morgan said these things to a freshman class at Yale, and he ended, "In short, he needs you."

And this brings me back to where I started, your importance to Brown University. You are our reason for being, not because you will listen passively and write down uncritically, but because without you there is no reason to speak or to write. What happens in the class-room is not the delivery of facts to whom it may concern, but the analysis of possibilities and probabilities by concerned people, teacher and students alike. Learning is not a passive process. A shy person cannot learn. An impatient person cannot teach. Learning is a shared experience. Without students, who is a teacher? More than the calf wants to suck the mother's milk, the cow wants to suckle that calf. I do not mean to suggest you have nothing to do but sit back, hear what a teacher has to say, and announce why he is wrong, or why you do not agree with him. That childish conception bears slight resemblance to what is to be done. I mean you have got to learn things for your part, and ask questions of your own perceptions, as much as of your teacher's: it is a shared quest, a collective skepticism.

What is the measure of success? How will you know, in June of 1976, whether you have wisely spent these four beautiful years?

First, you should have a good grasp of some specific field of learning, not solely the data of such a field, though they are important, but the way that field works, how people think within it, and why. You should know some specific thing, indeed, a great many specific things.

But, second, you also should have mastered three skills which mark the educated man and woman: how to listen attentively, and to think clearly, and to write accurately. No matter what you study at Brown, you should learn these three things. To be sure, the modes of thought and the means of writing or other expressions are going to differ from one field to the next. But in common they will exhibit concern for accuracy, clarity, precision, order, lucid argumentation.

And, third, you should feel slightly discontented, discontented with yourselves—therefore capable of continued growth; discontented with your field of work—therefore capable of critical judgment and improvement; discontented with the world at large— therefore capable of taking up the world's tasks as a personal and individual challenge.

So now you come not merely to spend four years in a world you have not made and for which you therefore do not bear responsibility. You come to join and build a community, a community of scholars. If the experience of community is meaningful to you, you will, wherever you may be, never really leave it. You will continue to participate in the scholarly enterprise: asking questions, finding answers, telling people about them.

INDEX